TV DOT COM

To Dennis !.
The future is now !
The opportunity to view !
Let's grab it . .
Mike Erwin
Age 200!

TV DOT COM

TV Books

NEW YORK

*The Future of
Interactive
Television*

Phillip Swann

Library of Congress Cataloging-in-Publication Data
Swann, Phillip.
TV dot com: how television is shaping our future /
Phillip Swann.
p. cm.
ISBN 1-57500-177-2 (pbk.)
1. Interactive television. 2. Interactive
television—Social aspects. I. Title.
TK6679.3. S93 2000
302.23'45—dc21
00-030274

TV Books, L.L.C.
1619 Broadway
New York, NY 10019
www.tvbooks.com

Interior design by Rachel Reiss

Manufactured in the
United States

Contents

For my Mom and Dad.

CHAPTER ONE

Interactive TV: Are You Ready?

Man's mind stretched to a new idea never goes back to its original dimensions.

—Oliver Wendell Holmes, Jr.

The prevailing wisdom among snobs and cynics in the late 1940s and early 1950s was that television was created for those poor saps who didn't have a life. Who *else* would sit in front of a box that flashed pictures of people so blurry that they looked like apparitions from a bad dream? Indeed, the images were so ghostlike that some viewers must have believed that the *Today Show*'s Dave Garroway had a twin brother who seemed to speak at the same time he did. The early TV viewer was further challenged when the horizontal-hold knob was inhabited by evil spirits, a daily if not hourly occurrence. I think I can say without fear of contradiction that nothing in the American cultural experience has ever produced more frustration than trying to watch a TV set whose picture continually floated from north to south, north to south, north to south. When as a kid I heard that Elvis Presley had shot out a television set, I immediately assumed that his horizontal-hold button had gone awry.

But America quickly fell in love with television, despite its cost, its early technical difficulties, and its bargain-basement production values. There was something comforting about coming home after a long day at work, switching on the set, and letting someone entertain you. It was like being a king under siege and, after a tough day on the battlefield, you could sit back and summon the court jesters to take your mind off the war. TV court jesters such as Milton Berle, Jackie Gleason, Lucille Ball, and Bob Hope soon became living room fixtures, perhaps more loved and welcomed than certain family members.

For years, there were only three channels—ABC, NBC, and CBS—but it didn't seem to matter to most people. In fact, for some, it was a blessing; all you had to do was take out your *TV Guide,* decide which channel you were going to watch that night, grab a beer, and plop your fanny into the chair. How much easier could it be?

After many years, though, there was some pent-up demand among TV owners for more channels. After all, they found it increasingly difficult to distinguish one network's programming from another. For instance, the plot lines for the 1960s sitcoms *Bewitched* and *I Dream of Jeannie* would basically vary only in character names and occupations. It was as if the writing team for *Bewitched* was moonlighting for *Jeannie,* or the other way around.

But, like nature, television abhors a vacuum. And in the 1980s, large men wearing ill-fitting jumpsuits entered our homes, pulled long white cables from odd holes they drilled in the wall, and connected them to the back of our televisions. They handed us something called a remote control and turned on the TV. Suddenly, there were dozens of channels to watch, everything from HBO to ESPN to maybe even the Playboy Channel when no one was looking. (Even if you didn't purchase a subscription to Playboy, what was going on behind those squiggly lines was sometimes more entertaining than ABC's prime-time lineup.) The impact of cable TV was instant and enormous. To cite just a few examples:

- With so many channels suddenly available—and a handy remote control at the ready—viewers could not resist surfing the dial. (In fact, the phrase "channel surfing" quickly became part of the vernacular.) One could certainly make a compelling argument that this behavior contributed to our nation's short-attention-span disorder, for which thousands of schoolkids are now being medicated. Few viewers today can sit through an entire program without picking up the remote and checking out another channel—at least during the show's commercial breaks. During the three-channel days, the average TV viewer may have kept the same channel on all night; it was too much trouble to get out of his chair to turn the dial. But today's viewer needs constant gratification: If she's not entertained or intrigued for any stretch of time, she will flip the dial.

- The increase in channels—plus the launch of the video rental store—led to Americans spending more time at home watching television. Sociologists searching for explanations behind the "cocooning" trend of the 1980s and 1990s don't have to look any further than the TV.

- To compete with new channels such as ESPN, the networks started throwing money at the professional sports leagues to ensure that they would include top-quality sporting events in their programming lineups. With the leagues making more money, the players began to demand their fair share. Consequently, player salaries soared beyond anyone's wildest dreams; make that "beyond anyone's wildest nightmares" if you have tried to buy a ticket lately. During the last two decades, the owners have steadily raised ticket prices to offset increases in player salaries. The bottom line is that there are more games on TV, but it's more difficult and expensive to attend them in person.

I could cite a hundred more ways that cable TV has changed our lives, but this book is about Interactive TV. So let's pose the question: If the launch of a fifty-channel cable TV system had such a profound and pervasive impact, what will happen when television offers five hundred channels—plus the ability to surf the Net, order products, pause live TV shows, play video games, and conduct video phone chats? What happens, in short, when Interactive TV becomes a reality?

Satisfy Your Desires

And it's going to happen, believe me. If you don't believe me, just listen to C. Michael Armstrong, the chairman of AT&T, the nation's largest cable and telephone company. Armstrong, the shrewd former head of General Motors, usually plays his cards so close to the vest that they wind up inside his shirt. But this is what he told the National Cable Television Association's annual conference in 1999: "The real news is the merger of technology. I'm not talking about a 'future world' exhibit at a World's Fair. This future will happen and it will happen in the next five years."

Big words—but they are backed by big money. Cable and satellite TV companies (and some of the telephone companies such as U.S. West) are spending billions of dollars to develop new digital set-top boxes that will scratch your every itch and satisfy your every desire. These new boxes will make your life more convenient, more fun, and, in many ways, more enriching. They will take you on adventures of the mind, bring you closer to friends and loved ones, perhaps even give you a greater sense of control and self-esteem. They will change your life in ways you can barely imagine.

Before bestowing the Nobel Prize on Armstrong and his colleagues, let me hasten to add that the driving motivation behind the development of digital TV is not at all altruistic. The titans of communications have a host of creative and dazzling new services they would like to sell you. However, they have concluded that they will generate more sales if they put these services on the TV. Why the TV rather than the personal computer?

Consumers are more comfortable with the TV than the PC, particularly at home. The TV conveys relaxation; the PC is associated with work. And every good salesperson knows that the more relaxed your customer is, the greater your chances of making the sale.

As of this writing, the PC is in approximately 40 percent of American homes, but the TV is in nearly every American home. In fact, most homes have two or three TVs. The TV is so pervasive in this country that chances are, if you visit the poorest family in the swamps of Louisiana, you'll find a rusted, thirteen-inch Philco sitting atop a cardboard box.

"The television is the three-thousand-pound gorilla," says Nicholas Donatiello, president of Odyssey, a market research firm in San Francisco. Even Microsoft, which once believed that the PC would dominate all things electronic, has changed its opinion and its marketing agenda. Microsoft is developing enhanced TV software that will be installed in millions of cable and satellite set-top boxes.

"Microsoft has recognized TV as a first-class business opportunity. We've broken out of the 'just the PC' thinking," says Phil Goldman, Microsoft's general manager of WebTV platforms and a cofounder of WebTV, Microsoft's Interactive TV set-top box. At this writing, the first-generation set-top boxes are rolling off the assembly lines at breakneck speed. In fact, as you read this, you may already have one. If not, and if you're a cable TV subscriber, expect a call soon from one of those burly chaps with the ill-fitting jumpsuits. In most cities, the early cable set-tops will feature a limited number of add-ons—you'll likely get some new channels and the new Electronic Programming Guide. (See Chapter

Four.) By 2001, however, the majority of cable TV operators will expand their lineups to include interactive shopping, the Internet on TV, and other dazzling advances. Why
will cable wait until 2001? I will try not to bore you with
technical details in this book, but suffice it to say that cable's
set-top boxes are expected to have a greater capacity at that
time. If you're curious to learn more, go on the Net and do
a search for "Broadband"—hits will lead you to scores of
documents explaining the fine points of bandwidth and
other fascinating (or abstruse) technical issues.

Interactive TV companies are also fearful of scaring consumers if they offer too many features at first. After all, they
are targeting an audience that finds programming a VCR to
be an algebraic equation. If the average TV viewer is met
with five new interactive features at once, all of which require some education before implementing, there's a good
chance that that new set-top box will wind up in the trash.
"You want the kind of dynamic service which doesn't make
people feel stupid, where the consumer faces a few choices
at any one time [when] viewing the services," says Mark
Potter, head of Oracle's Interactive TV division. "The consumer demand for this is incredible, so much more than
what people had hoped for. You have to come out of the
gate with a variety of applications, but in order to nurture
that demand, the applications must be high-quality and
backed by solid customer service."

But in the brave new world of digital TV, both cable and
satellite television will eventually become so advanced that
they will seem almost prescient in their ability to give you
what you want, when you want it, and how you want it. You

will be able to toss your PC and use your TV as an Internet appliance; you will be able to discard your VCR and order your TV to record shows; you will be able to change the camera angles of sporting events; you will be able to pause a live TV show and take a phone call without missing any of the action. You'll be able to do almost anything your mind can think of.

"This is just like when black-and-white TV went to color," says Microsoft's Goldman. "We're going to be looking back at the twentieth century and at how quaint and old-fashioned TV was."

I Want My ITV

The phrase *Interactive TV* may sound familiar to you. After all, this is not the first time that big media have tried to bring ITV to America. Time Warner conducted an Interactive TV experiment in Orlando from 1994 to 1997, and it was a huge flop. But TW, which offered movies on demand and e-mail, acknowledges that its technology at the time was not up to the task. If consumers are going to be promised interactivity, it had better be fast, instant, and without error. Time Warner's experiment was anything but that. Still, many following the ITV movement questioned whether consumers really wanted it.

However, research shows that consumers at the dawn of the twenty-first century have a different way of thinking about television than they did even six or seven years ago. Many networks today encourage their viewers to interact with shows by going to their web sites, where they can learn more about the show, view background documents or images, or participate in a related chat or poll. Yahoo!, the web search portal, conducted a study in 1999 that showed that about half of U.S. households have a television and computer in the same room, with the majority being kept on at the same time. Showtime, the premium movie/sports channel, did a similar poll that showed that many viewers are interacting with the TV shows while on their PC. In addition, over the last few years, the networks have added a number of graphics to the screen such as channel logos and scoreboards during sporting events. Viewers have become accustomed to seeing something on the screen other than the show. From there, it's a short leap for the networks to insert an on-screen icon that would allow the viewer to interact with the show by clicking on it; the "middleman"—the personal computer—is eliminated.

"A highly habituated online home is ready to think about practicing online in other appliances, TV being one," Barry Schuler, president of America Online's Interactive Services, told *Cablevision Magazine*. "But they don't want the TV becoming a big computer monitor with a keyboard. By itself, viewing a web page is not a wonderful thing. But applications like e-mail, instant messaging and other ways people can be with each other can help tie a home experience with a community experience. That's what will make TV explode into an active medium from a passive medium over the next decade."

"Interactive TV has gone from being a laughing stock to becoming a potentially massive revenue generator," adds

Josh Bernoff, an analyst at Forrester Research, Inc., which studies telecommunications trends.

So, the time is right. But are *you* ready? In the following chapters, I will examine the various features of Interactive TV and show how they will change just about everything we do—sometimes not necessarily for the better. Chapter Ten, for instance, will touch on how ITV could pose a threat to your privacy. In each chapter, I will also make some predictions for each ITV feature. Don't worry where your remote is right now—read on . . .

Predictions

▪ *1.*

Interactive TV (ITV) will be in every American home by the year 2010. The growth of ITV will be slow but steady. Many Americans still think of television as a passive experience, and they will have to be educated on the benefits of interacting with their sets. However, the education campaign has been under way for some time. By using the remote control, viewers have learned that they can gain a measure of control over what they watch by changing the channel. Before the "zapper" was available, viewers rarely "interacted" with their sets because it was too much trouble to get up and change the dial. In addition, networks such as NBC, ABC, and MTV have been encouraging their audiences to interact with shows via their web sites. ABC, for example, has heavily promoted its "Enhanced TV" site during broadcasts of major sporting events. The site offers real-time stats from the game, plus opportunities to participate in game-related surveys. ABC's "Enhanced TV" page attracted 650,000 users during Super Bowl XXXIV, which was won by the St. Louis Rams. In a survey conducted by ABC, 96 percent of viewers who visited the Enhanced TV site said they would do it again in the future. "These impressive figures reaffirm the coming of age of convergent programming," says Jonathan Leess, executive producer of ABC's Enhanced TV division.

2.

Several ITV companies, ranging from AOL/Time Warner to Microsoft, will launch massive marketing and public relations campaigns to educate Americans about ITV's benefits. The campaigns will be designed to convince consumers that ITV features will make their lives more convenient and more fun. The marketing effort will be pivotal to persuading Americans—most of whom still have trouble even setting the clock on their VCRs—to give new products and services a try. Companies that fail to understand the need for this education campaign will come up short and become high-tech dinosaurs.

3.

At first, cable and satellite TV companies will offer Interactive TV services at discounted prices to attract new customers. For example, the local cable company might offer an Internet TV service at a monthly rate lower than the average Internet Service Provider. The idea would be to get consumers to give the new service a try.

4.

By the year 2002, approximately fifteen million homes will use at least one Interactive TV feature, whether it's the Personal Video Recorder (PVR), the Electronic Programming Guide (EPG), or an Internet TV set-top box. Thanks to positive word-of-mouth and effective marketing campaigns, the number will quickly soar to forty million by 2004.

5.

The merger of America Online and Time Warner at the dawn of the new millennium will go down in history as the deal that put ITV on the map (even though Microsoft had already spent hundreds of millions of dollars developing and marketing ITV features in its WebTV set-top box). AOL and Time Warner will combine their considerable resources to create a dazzling array of interactive products and services, everything from TV set-top boxes to TV shows that offer instant links to related web sites. Concerned that AOL and Time Warner will dominate the ITV market, nearly every major media company will invest a large chunk of its budget on ITV projects; no one, they believe, can afford to be left behind in the world of digital TV. The effort to keep pace with AOL/Time Warner will act as a catalyst to speed up the ITV movement. Jim McDonald, CEO of Scientific Atlanta, a maker of digital cable TV boxes, told *USA Today* that "Interactive TV got moved up a couple of years." (Previously, most media companies felt they could wait on ITV because Microsoft was pretty much the only player—and they were having limited success with WebTV. However, the combination of AOL's Internet resources and Time Warner's entertainment stable virtually guarantees that the merged monolith will develop a dynamic Interactive TV business.)

6.

Leading players in the ITV industry will include AOL/Time Warner; Microsoft (and WebTV); Sony; AT&T; TiVo, Replay TV (Personal Video Recorder makers); NBC; *TV Guide;* ABC/Disney/ESPN; Blockbuster Video; MTV; Wink (a company that makes software enabling viewers to order products on their TV screen); Motorola/General Instrument and Scientific Atlanta (makers of digital cable TV set-top boxes); as well as DIRECTV and The Dish Network, the two satellite TV operators.

7.

The first major ITV success story will be the Personal Video Recorder, which permits consumers to pause and record TV shows without using a videocassette recorder. Consumers will quickly embrace the PVR because it makes their lives more convenient. In addition, the PVR is essentially an upgrade of the VCR; unlike Net TV—surfing the Internet on television—the PVR doesn't require consumers to think about an entirely new way to use their televisions.

8.

Another early success story: the Electronic Programming Guide. The EPG provides a week of program listings on your TV screen that can be searched by actor, title, or genre. The EPG, which will be available on all-new set-top boxes accessible by either satellite or digital cable, will soon render obsolete the traditional printed television guide.

9.

However, *TV Guide,* the king of printed guides, has shrewdly invested millions in developing its own EPG technology and will become a leader in the new category.

10.

High Definition TV (HDTV) will struggle to reach a mass audience in the next decade. The delivery of an HDTV channel requires a massive amount of bandwidth on a cable or satellite system. The cable companies will prefer to use their available bandwidth to provide more TV channels and interactive features, which can generate more e-commerce and advertising revenue than HDTV. "The original intent was to provide HDTV over the digital signal so the public could have a clear transmission and better picture," James Boyle, vice president of First Union Securities, which tracks the broadcasting industry, told *Interactive Week* magazine. "But the problem is that advertisers aren't going to pay more for HDTV vs. enhanced analog transmissions. If a television station tells an advertiser that it has to pay 20 percent more so that customers can see the ad a little better, the advertiser is going to laugh. Advertisers don't care if it's a better picture, because all they're paying for is eyeballs." The sudden availability of more channels and convenient interactive features will also dampen consumer demand for HDTV; consumers will become preoccupied with the new features and thus less likely to be curious about HDTV.

11.

Sales of big-screen TVs will soar in the next several years, when customers realize they need a larger screen to read text on their TV, such as articles from web sites and EPG listings. This will also encourage people to buy new digital TVs, which feature larger screens and crisper pictures.

12.

Sales of satellite TV dishes will begin to slow (except perhaps in rural areas) when cable TV adds more channels and interactive features. Satellite TV enjoyed a boom in the second half of the 1990s largely because it had the bandwidth to offer three times the number of channels that a cable operator could. However, the digital cable set-top box will permit cable TV to match satellite TV channel for channel.

13.

To stay competitive, satellite TV companies will need to develop a considerable amount of original, exclusive programming (movies, sports, specials, and so on) as well as unique interactive services. In addition, satellite providers will make room for more HDTV channels, to help distinguish themselves from cable TV's lineup.

14.

The TV will not replace the PC. For instance, it's hard to envision a viewer working on an Excel spreadsheet on his TV. "Initially we looked at the TV as an available monitor," WebTV marketing director Rob Schoeben told *USA Today*. "But we realized that we missed a fundamental point. That [TV] monitor is a TV set and people want it to be a better TV, not an alternative to the PC." However, when PC features such as Internet browsing start to migrate to the TV, PC software companies will need to develop more programs that are best used on the PC or that enhance what's on television.

15.

The television will become a home networking center, enabling consumers to control all their electronic products and household appliances with the remote control. By example, a viewer could be watching a TV show and cooking dinner when she remembers she forgot to turn on the backyard sprinkler. With the touch of a button, the sprinkler will begin to water the yard. "Even things like the washing machine, when it's done with a task, will be able to send a notification," says Microsoft chief Bill Gates. "I actually have a home like that and it really works." Home networking systems are expected to be installed in ten million homes by 2003, according to Yankee Group, a research firm.

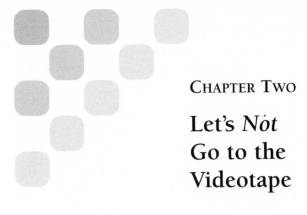

CHAPTER TWO

Let's *Not* Go to the Videotape

Technology makes it possible for people to gain control over everything, except over technology.
—John Tudor

In the late 1970s, the first videocassette recorder made its way into retail stores across the nation. The first thing you noticed about it was its size. It was big. When the store clerk asked whether you needed assistance in bringing a newly purchased VCR to your car . . . well, he wouldn't ask. He knew that you would. Despite its girth and clunky features—the cassette tray opened with such force that it would scare small children and threaten to impale anyone who got too close—the first VCR represented a scientific breakthrough. For the first time, you could record a show or sporting event from your television and replay it over and over. You could also rent or purchase a prerecorded movie or show and watch it whenever you felt like it. (Of course, the killjoys at Blockbuster and other video rental outlets soon instituted the "late fee," which was quickly followed by the insane "You didn't rewind your tape!!!" charge. Even today, it's difficult to believe that the life of a twenty-year-old video rental clerk is so full that she can't take a few minutes to rewind a tape.)

Some two decades later, it is easy to be jaded about the invention of the VCR. But at the time, it seemed as if a magical box had dropped from the heavens. It answered the prayers of millions of people who had grown weary of being at the mercy of network schedulers. Previously, loyal viewers had been forced to rearrange their lives so that they could watch their favorite shows at their scheduled times; if they had to work late or got caught in traffic, they would miss the show and would have to wait until it aired again as a summer repeat. But the VCR gave the TV viewer a measure of control.

I say "measure of control" because there was a small catch: You had to figure out how to program a VCR—a daunting task for even the most technically inclined. My first VCR included a small "programming stick," which you were supposed to insert into a narrow opening in the front of the deck. Then, you were instructed to wiggle the stick to manipulate a lever that allegedly set your VCR's programming clock to record at your requested time. The process took the steady hand and patience of an international jewel thief. More often than not, I made sure I was home at the beginning of a show I wanted to record so that I could manually hit the "Record" button. Later VCR models offered improvements on the programming feature. But

Americans are not as tech-savvy as some might have you believe, particularly older Americans who didn't grow up in the PC generation. Many people are still stumped about how to set the clock on their VCR. In fact, if an alien visited the average TV family, he would leave thinking that it is always twelve o'clock.

VCR manufacturers and other companies have struggled for the past two decades to solve this problem once and for all. Probably the best known of the products designed to take VCR owners out of their misery is Gemstar's VCR Plus. The VCR Plus, which is installed in many higher-priced VCRs, will record a show if you punch in a programming code that extends roughly from Maine to Butte, Montana. Seemingly just adding to the viewer's confusion, the VCR Plus has had limited success despite the fact that its codes are ubiquitous in local and national television guides. For instance, here's a sample VCR Plus listing from the *Los Angeles Times'* television guide of February 6, 2000: "54 The Sundance Channel Movie: I Think I Do (6:25) 36492132."

The "36492132" is the VCR Plus code. If you punch those numbers into a VCR Plus–enabled VCR, it will automatically tape the show. There is no need to program your VCR to start recording at 6:25 P.M. or even to instruct your VCR to record the Sundance Channel. The VCR Plus is a good try, but it's tantamount to replacing one technical headache for another. Who wants to scribble down an eight-digit number, which, by the way, is printed in visually-challenging six-point type on newsprint, and then punch those numbers one by one into a VCR? All of that just to tape *I Think I Do*? I think I won't.

The Personal Video Recorder

For years, marketing research has indicated that consumers wanted a product that would enable them to record TV shows with one step, not two, three, or twelve. The research also showed that many people would like to have a video recorder that doesn't require videotape; stacks of unwatched videotapes are nearly as large a contributor to living room clutter as unread magazines and newspapers. But the demand for these features seemed to be no more than idle daydreaming until 1999 when two Silicon Valley companies, TiVo and ReplayTV, launched the Personal Video Recorder. (The first PVR was a separate set-top box that was sold at retail. However, cable TV companies will soon be adding PVR features to their digital cable set-tops. DIRECTV and The Dish Network, the two satellite TV operators, have already included the PVR in higher-end receivers.) The PVR has a hard disc drive inside that digitally records every show that's on your television— whether you are watching that show or not, or whether you have even instructed the PVR to record it. For example, let's say you turn on your TV and discover that your favorite movie of all time is on but it began ten minutes ago. By hitting the Fast Rewind button, you could go back to the beginning of the movie in literally two or three seconds. It's like being in a time machine. The PVR also has the capacity to pause live or recorded programming with the touch of a button, and certain models can digitally store up to thirty hours of programming. Are you amazed yet? Well, how about this: The PVR also comes with an on-screen listings guide that enables you to instruct the PVR to record a program by clicking on its grid and then clicking on the Record button. What does a PVR *not* do? Well, it doesn't require you to punch in eight numbers, wiggle a stick at it, or stand on your head.

Surprisingly, the launch of the PVR went largely unnoticed by most Americans in 1999. The dot-com craze dominated the business and technology sections of the local newspaper because of its influence on the stock market. However, in time, the PVR will have more influence on the TV industry than any new advance in television since color. If that seems like a bold statement, let me offer this illustration of how a PVR gives the TV viewer control over what he watches and when he watches it. It's the first week of the 2001 NFL season. Joe Sixpack is watching a live broadcast of a National Football League game between the St. Louis Rams and the Green Bay Packers. The game is tied 17–17 midway through the third quarter, but the Rams are driving deep into Packer territory. As the Rams break huddle at the Packer 27-yard line, Joe's phone rings. In past seasons, Joe would do one of two things in this situation: (1) He would ignore the call and let his answering machine pick it up, or (2) he would take the call and begin to curse the person on the other end of the line for having the audacity for interrupting him during a big game. But today, Joe has another option. He picks up his remote control and hits the pause button just as St. Louis quarterback Kurt Warner takes the snap from center. Suddenly, it's like that *Twilight Zone* episode in which someone was able to freeze all pedestrian traffic by snapping his fingers; every player on the screen is frozen in the moment. Joe puts down the remote and runs over to pick up the phone—it's a long-lost buddy whom he hasn't spoken to in years. Knowing that he won't miss a play of the game, Joe doesn't feel rushed to end the call at the first opportunity. He learns that his friend has moved back to the neighborhood, and they make plans to get together. Twenty minutes after the call begins, Joe says good-bye and hangs up. With a big smile on his face, he walks to the kitchen, grabs a beer, and plops back into his easy chair. He hits the pause button to unfreeze the picture, and Warner immediately starts to drop back into the pocket. The quarterback dodges a Packer lineman and hits wide receiver Issac Bruce over the middle for a twelve-yard gain to bring the Rams to the Packer fifteen-yard line. Since the live action is actually twenty minutes ahead, Joe decides he will catch up. As the Rams huddle, Joe hits another button on his remote that enables him to skip over seven seconds of the game; the Rams are now set at the line of scrimmage for the next play. Warner takes the snap and hands off to running back Marshall Faulk, who dashes up the middle for a touchdown. After the extra point, the network takes a two-minute commercial break, but Joe hits the thirty-second skip-forward button four times and leaves the advertisers in the dust. By continuing to use the PVR's fast forward feature, Joe eventually returns to live action. He didn't miss a single play; he got to talk to his old buddy; *and* he eliminated the commercials and the dead-time "action" in between plays.

"Never Watch Live TV"

For five decades, since television became a fixture in many American homes in the 1950s, the networks banked on the concept that most people will pay at least some attention to the commercials that air during a show. Sure, the VCR allows you to zip past a commercial during a prerecorded show. But the process is cumbersome at best—and even when you hit the fast-forward button, you can still see the commercial on the screen, albeit in fast motion. However, the PVR's fast-forward button zaps the commercial as if it never existed. It's easy to see how addictive that can be. Many viewers will watch recorded versions of their favorite shows so that they can eliminate the commercials and save time. "We give consumers a half-dozen ways to navigate the seven thousand hours of programming a day," says Stacy Jolna, TiVo's vice president of programming. Josh Bernoff, an analyst with Forrester Research, predicts that the PVR will lead to consumers watching 8 percent fewer commercials by 2005 and 50 percent fewer by the end of the decade. "It's phenomenal how good it is," Loren Finkelstein, an early PVR user, told the Associated Press early in the year 2000. "I never watch live TV." Of course, this is not a comforting notion for network salespeople or advertising agencies that spend long hours and vast sums of money creating spots that consumers will remember. At first, the networks made noises as if they planned to storm Silicon Valley and invade the general headquarters of TiVo and ReplayTV. Lawsuits were filed for various reasons, but almost before the ink dried on the legal papers the networks decided to invest millions of dollars in the PVR firms. It was a classic case of "If you can't beat 'em, buy 'em." The networks saw that it would be easier to influence what the PVR companies do if they owned part of the store. (See "Predictions.") "They're anxious to work with us to develop that next step. It's like one door closes and another one opens," says TiVo's Jolna.

Now, even NBC network chief Robert Wright admits to using a TiVo at his home. "I don't think we have anything to be afraid of." But he does wonder about people who store hours and hours of shows. "The problem is when are you going to watch them?"

Predictions

▪ *1.*

Millions of Americans will swap their VCRs for either a new Personal Video Recorder set-top box or a cable TV or satellite TV box that comes equipped with the PVR feature. The PVR will become the fastest growing product in consumer electronics history, exceeding the compact disc player and the mini-satellite dish. It will be in every American household by the year 2006.

▪ *2.*

ReplayTV, TiVo, and other manufacturers of Personal Video Recorders will become industry giants overnight. The advertising community and the networks will have to work closely with PVR makers to ensure that they get their message to viewers.

▪ *3.*

Viewers will soon learn the fine art of "pause-surfing"— freezing a live show for a few minutes so that they can check their e-mail, surf the Net, take a phone call, or buy something. The convenience of pausing a live show—as well as the temptation of using other interactive features—will lead to fewer occasions where people sit down and watch a show from beginning to end without interruption. People will start watching TV shows the way they read books: a little at a time.

■ **4.**

The VCR will still be useful in the early years of the PVR. Viewers will make conventional videotapes of shows they have stored on the PVR's hard drive, as archives. But as the technology evolves, the capacity of the PVR's hard drive will expand to permit consumers to store dozens of hours of programming. Eventually, the VCR will be shelved forever.

■ **5.**

In a few years, viewers will be able to e-mail their favorite shows to friends and loved ones just as they used to trade videotapes and as they now e-mail family photos. They will also start making digital copies of their videotape libraries so that they can be seen on their PVR, without ever losing any more fidelity (magnetic tapes decay).

■ **6.**

Sports broadcasts will cut back on their use of the instant replay, because viewers at home will have the ability to perform the same task on their PVR. Color commentators will spend more time discussing what might happen next rather than what happened previously.

▪ 7.

The concept of "appointment television"—arranging to be home at a precise time to watch a particular program—will soon become a thing of the past. Thanks to the PVR and Video On Demand services, the average viewer will learn that she can watch shows *when* she wants and *how* she wants. She can skip commercials, fast forward shows at blinding speeds, or pause them. The consumer's ability to control her viewing schedule will place greater pressure on the networks to work with advertisers to ensure that their message is effectively delivered to a wide audience.

▪ 8.

The PVR feature that permits the user to skip commercials with the touch of a button will come under fire from advertisers and the networks. However, consumers will quickly embrace the feature and resist efforts to have it removed. This will leave the networks and the PVR manufacturers in a tight spot—they will need to appease the advertising community, but they will also need to satisfy consumer demand. Regardless of how the debate is resolved, the networks will have to offer advertisers a variety of new ways to deliver their message, including product placement in shows and spots on PVR menus and Electronic Programming Guide grids.

▪ 9.

The TV commercial, as we know it, will not fade away. Rather, companies will have to invest more money in creating entertaining commercials that viewers will want to watch. In addition, companies will need to create a public relations buzz around commercials to attract the viewer's attention. The model: Super Bowl commercials, which sometimes are more interesting than the actual game. Companies that air Super Bowl spots spend considerable time and money to make sure the viewer is aware of the commercial even before he sees it. Through PVR menu spots, web site banners, PR blitzes, product placement on TV shows, and "teasers" broadcast by on-air network talent, an advertiser can alert the viewer that its commercial is worth watching.

▪ *10.*

The Nielsen ratings will be dramatically restructured. Shows will be rated not only by how many people watched them in their time slots, but also by how many people downloaded them on their PVRs for later viewing.

▪ *11.*

The networks will start broadcasting more live shows (like the gripping nuclear-war drama *Fail Safe,* broadcast in April 2000) to encourage people to tune in at that time rather than recording it for later viewing. The show will have to seem so special that people can't wait to watch it.

CHAPTER THREE

Do You Want to Buy Ally McBeal's Skirt?

Advertisers are the interpreters of our dreams. Like the movies they infect the routine futility of our days with purposeful adventure. Their weapons are our weaknesses: fear, ambition, illness, pride, selfishness, desire and ignorance. And these weapons must be kept as bright as a sword.

—*E. B. White*

The television commercial can be annoying, useful, entertaining, and, sometimes, more influential than any prime-time TV show. Who can forget how Walter Mondale sliced up rival Gary Hart in the 1984 Democratic presidential race when he asked, "Where's the beef?," a suggestion that Hart's "New Ideas" campaign was without substance. Mondale, a former vice president and one of the most respected statesmen of the post–World War II generation, won his party's nomination in large part because he repeated a popular catch-line from a hamburger ad.

The TV commercial has the potential to have that kind of influence, because we see it over and over. Many spots for necessity items such as food, toilet paper, soft drinks, and beer (a necessity in this country) air nearly every night, sometimes two or three times a night. The commercial's punch line gets stuck in our head like a song that continually plays on the radio. It's not that we particularly like the commercial or are struck by its message, it's just that we can't erase it from our feeble brains. The problem is compounded when we venture into society and find others having the same problem—within seconds, the commercial's slogan pops into the conversation: "It just keeps going and going . . ." (Energizer batteries). "It takes a licking and keeps on ticking" (Timex watches). "I can't believe I ate the whole thing" (Alka-Seltzer). "Whassup!" (Budweiser). The catchphrase is used as social shorthand—by repeating a well-known line, people can instantly bond. Consequently, it doesn't take long for the catchphrase to spread across the land like the black plague. (The line "Show me the money!" from the 1996 film *Jerry Maguire* is a good example of how the nation can become fixated on a simple series of words. Many Americans still use the phrase when asked if they think someone will make a fair offer.) Of course, nothing makes an advertiser happier than to see Americans go over the cliff like lemmings, humming a popular TV commercial slogan or jingle. The advertiser is not concerned with cultural blight or behavioral conformity; he just wants to sell his product. If America turns into a nation of robots—

all buzzing the same phrase over and over—well, so be it. How are sales?

However, as we noted in Chapter Two, the TV commercial may have met its match in the Personal Video Recorder. The PVR allows a viewer to skip over a commercial in a PVR-recorded show. The feature is so easy to use—and so convenient—that industry analysts are predicting that many viewers will stop watching live TV entirely; they will record everything so that they can zap out the commercials. Of course, the TV commercial will not die—far from it, in fact. Madison Avenue will develop new campaigns designed to keep the viewer's trigger finger off the zap button. (See "Predictions.") But it seems likely that viewers will watch fewer commercials and, perhaps more important, remember fewer still. It will be more difficult for an advertiser to implant a catchphrase in the brain of the American consumer. How many people would have asked "Where's the beef?" if they had seen the Wendy's ad one time instead of a hundred?

But cry not for advertisers. Interactive TV will be the best thing that ever happened to them. The reason is interactive shopping.

Cable and satellite TV operators are installing software in their new digital set-top boxes that will enable viewers to order goods and services right on screen. The software, developed by Interactive TV companies such as Microsoft's WebTV, Wink, and Open TV, will let the networks transmit interactive messages along with their broadcasts. (For you techies out there, the networks send the messages through what's called the vertical blanking system—the same place where closed-captioning titles are transmitted.) The messages will pop up in the form of icons that will blink in the corner of the screen during certain parts of a show. When the viewer clicks on an icon, he will be given the opportunity to buy a product that has something to do with the program he is watching. The message also could link the viewer to the network's web site where he could get more information about the show. For example, if you were watching a MSNBC report on airline safety, the news network could transmit an icon that would transport the viewer to a web site, which has an archive of past Associated Press stories on airline crashes. The icon also could open up an on-screen chat room for the show—although anyone who has ever been in a chat room knows that the room's actual topic is rarely discussed.

"We're not solving world hunger here, but we are offering American consumers an easy and free way to interact with their television using nothing more than their good old remote control," says Maggie Wilderotter, Wink's chief executive officer.

Wilderotter may not be solving world hunger, but her software—and the software of her competitors—will serve up a feast for all those invited. Interactive shopping will generate billions in sales for advertisers, the networks, and the cable and satellite TV operators. Yes, billions. How can I say that? Let me count the ways:

1. Some social critics who haven't had an original thought since the Carter administration say the TV viewer is nothing more than a Couch Potato—a

lazy, passive blob who has no interest in interacting with the screen. Well, that may have been true twenty years ago when you could only watch three or four channels—and you had to get up from your couch or easy chair to turn the channel. But cable TV and the remote control changed all that. Many viewers, particularly males, now interact with their screens about every ten seconds, flipping from one channel to the next. The "Couch Potato" has been replaced by "Short Attention Span Man" (most women seem immune to this affliction). You won't have to persuade him to start clicking. In addition, many adults in their twenties and early thirties grew up using a personal computer; they are comfortable with the idea of interacting with the screen, whether it's a PC screen or a TV screen. "With enhanced advertising, we deliver a message that combines the emotional power of television with the interactive capabilities of the Internet," says Jan Klug, a marketing communications manager for Ford, which has produced Interactive TV commercials for the broadcast of the Grammys and other special events. "We have developed an advertising experience that will appeal to young consumers who have grown up with the Internet."

2. And speaking of the Net, online shopping sites are generating hundreds of millions in sales. What will happen when Americans can shop via the TV rather than the PC? Well, a Gallup/Pace Micro Technology

study found that 42 percent of consumers would feel more comfortable using the television for home shopping, while just 26 percent of respondents stated a preference for the PC. And this study was taken in 1999 when only one million people—the WebTV audience—could surf the Net on TV! In addition, early research by WebTV found that 49 percent of its subscribers had purchased a service or product online. The average WebTV owner spends 14.6 hours a week online via the TV, compared to roughly 12 hours a week for the PC owner.

3. The TV audience is a captive audience—you can't miss that little icon popping up on your screen. But TV merchandisers have an even more powerful weapon at their disposal—the emotional involvement of the TV viewer. For instance, let's say that after a climactic touchdown by the home team the network transmits an icon that lets you buy the team's official jersey or T-shirt. The fan may be so infused with team spirit that she can't resist buying the shirt—it will make her feel like she's part of the team.

Likewise, the network broadcasting a show featuring a female hero could send an icon that lets a loyal fan buy a related product right after the star is involved in a dramatic moment. For instance, let's say you are a woman watching your favorite show, *Ally McBeal*. Calista Flockhart, the calorically-challenged actress who plays Ally, is addressing the judge in a courtroom scene. Calista is wearing a short black skirt that happens to catch your fancy. "I love her clothes; I wonder where she gets them," you think to yourself. Suddenly, a small icon winks at you from the right-hand corner of the screen. You pick up your remote control, you hit the Enter button, and a message appears at the bottom of the screen: "Would You Like to Buy Ally's Skirt?" Despite a small fear that someone has invaded your thoughts, you click on the Yes button and another message reveals the skirt's designer and price. "Would You Like to Purchase This Item?" the screen asks. You look at Ally as if you were looking for advice; she's making eye contact with a cute guy in the courtroom, and the camera shows the guy looking her up and down—getting a particularly good look at . . . Ally's skirt. "Yes," you say to yourself. "I want to buy Ally McBeal's skirt! I want that guy in the courtroom!" You hit the Yes button, and the skirt will be delivered to you within forty-eight hours. (You submitted your credit card number and other miscellaneous information, such as clothing sizes and buying preferences, when you signed up with your cable or satellite TV service. They will know exactly which skirt to send you.)

"Enhanced TV is the next big step for advertisers. It enables a real-time exchange of valuable information between our clients and their consumers and it creates new opportunities to communicate in an interactive, one-to-one way to the TV audience," says Andy Prakken, executive director of communications services for the J. Walter Thompson advertising agency. "We know there will soon be an explosion in the number of homes capable of receiving interactive advertising. . . . We are pushing the envelope with new technologies that truly engage consumers."

Of course, it may be a few years before the networks decide to interrupt prime-time dramas with on-screen shopping overtures. Many viewers would rebel if the first
shopping icons popped up in the middle of an absorbing
movie, let's say. It would be wiser if the networks introduced the concept during sporting events, game shows,
and variety shows, which lend themselves to interruptions.
But TV executives are clearly contemplating how they can
customize their shows to make them more conducive to
online sales. Late in 1999, NBC announced that it would
sell on its web site a variety of jewelry and clothing "in-
spired" by its daytime soap opera *Passions.* NBC Internet
President Edmond Sanctis said he wouldn't rule out similar efforts with other NBC shows, including those in prime
time, to help "build commerce opportunities" into programming. I'm sure his words put a chill in the hearts of
TV writers all over Los Angeles, but the networks realize
that they could be sitting on a pot of gold. Using the *Ally
McBeal* example, Fox could cut a deal with K-Mart that
would give the retail giant three interactive shopping icons
during the one-hour shows. The icons would permit viewers to purchase K-Mart clothing worn by members of the
cast. (Those words may have put a chill in the hearts of actors and actresses all over Los Angeles.) K-Mart and Fox
would split the profits from all sales generated by the icons.
It would be a great deal for K-Mart. Why would it spend
millions on a national advertising campaign when instead
it could induce someone to buy its products with a care-
fully placed interactive link in a hit TV show? Why try to
sell clothes paraded by unknown models, rather than those

worn in gripping or hilarious scenes by actors whom viewers love and identify with?

"I really do believe that there is a new convergence between information, entertainment and direct selling. Once you have the technology for interactivity, you can have direct selling and you can bypass the middleman," USA Networks chief Barry Diller told the *New York Times* in 1999.

In the early stages of interactive shopping, the networks and the cable and satellite TV operators will likely focus on providing viewers with opportunities to buy items that they are accustomed to purchasing online or having delivered. For example, Domino's and WebTV in 1999 sponsored a *Star Trek* marathon on the local UPN affiliate in San Francisco. An interactive icon periodically appeared that enabled the viewer to order a free pizza by just clicking on the remote. Approximately 14 percent of the WebTV audience bit on the offer, but in a follow-up survey, 96 percent said they would be inclined to buy pizza via the TV in the future. And, as of this writing, Food.com and WebTV were developing an interactive program that would permit WebTV owners to order restaurant food directly through their TV. "Just as consumers today reach for the *TV Guide* to plan their evening entertainment, WebTV viewers can look to Food.com's site to plan and order their meals with just a few clicks of the remote control," says Karen Orton, vice president of business development at Food.com. "Conducting commerce from the living room couch will become as natural as dialing the phone, but with less hassle."

Predictions

■ *1.*

Online shopping, which experienced a boom in the late 1990s, will become a major force in the world of commerce when Americans can order goods and services on their TV sets. Within a decade or less, online shopping sites in such categories as books, music, movie rentals, toys, and household items will surpass their brick-and-mortar rivals in overall sales. In addition, in the next twenty years, television could become the nation's number one sales sector—more money may exchange hands on TV than any other outlet, including the retail store.

■ *2.*

The early success story of e-commerce on television: pizza delivery. The ease of ordering a pizza with a couple of touches on the remote control will prove irresistible to millions of Americans. Plus, consumers are already accustomed to ordering pizza from home. The ability to do it on television—without having to make a phone call— will be a boon for the Dominos of the world. Couch Potatoes morph into Couch Pepperoni!

■ *3.*

The convenience of buying items from your easy chair will put more pressure on retailers to find ways to lure consumers into the store. Many retail stores will become entertainment/community centers where people go for social reasons rather than just to buy something. Despite the ease of online buying, it does not provide the "personal touch" of shopping in person. Retailers will take advantage of that by increasing the social aspects of shopping offline.

4.

The dramatic increase in online sales will eventually lead to a national controversy over what critics will see as a manipulation of the TV viewer. Congressional and religious leaders will register alarm that the "lower class" is more susceptible to TV e-commerce pitches—and less able to pay the large credit card bills incurred from online buying. The debate will result in some safeguards that will protect the consumer, although the networks will still have far-reaching authority to practice e-commerce.

5.

The networks will start pressuring the creative community to increase the placement of brand name products in hit shows. Depending on the type of product, the placement will be either subliminal or blatant. Following the show's airing, viewers will be encouraged via advertisements and e-mails to order these products from either the network's or advertiser's web site. The network and the advertiser will split the proceeds from any online sales.

6.

Producers of TV shows that are not well suited for e-commerce tie-ins will have greater difficulty getting their programs on the air. Network executives will be less likely to give the green light to a show that cannot generate ancillary income via the selling of related products. For example, *Homicide,* the canceled NBC detective show set in Baltimore, was a likely suspect for termination every year during its run because of low ratings and gritty storylines. However, in the era of e-commerce, *Homicide's* creators would also have to battle against network executives in charge of online sales. Because of the show's content, *Homicide* would have little or no e-commerce potential— you can't exactly sell guns on TV. Consequently, *Homicide's* producers would have a greater burden to prove it would do well in the ratings and bring in advertising dollars.

7.

The networks will add more variety shows, sports shows, and game shows to their prime-time lineups, because those shows are well suited for e-commerce.

8.

The power of the e-commerce divisions at the networks will create a tremendous backlash in TV's artistic community. Studios will urge writers and directors to develop interactive content for the new medium. At first, many writers and directors will balk at changing their "artistic vision" to incorporate interactive features. "You want me to put what, where?" will be a common lament when they are asked to approve an interactive icon in the corner of a frame of a film or TV show. However, most writers and directors will eventually give in because they will see the benefits—both artistically and commercially—of developing interactive content. It will allow them to stretch their creativity in new ways and reach new audiences. Artists who fail to see "the benefits" will bring their stories to other mediums, such as web sites that offer Video On Demand.

■ **9.**

The growth of e-commerce on television will also lead to fears that the networks, cable and satellite TV companies, and other communications companies are becoming too powerful. Congress and the Justice Department will seek greater restrictions on TV-related companies, similar to the Justice Department's action against Microsoft in the late 1990s.

■ **10.**

Home shopping channels such as QVC will enjoy an initial surge in popularity as more viewers become accustomed to ordering goods via their TVs. However, in time, the home shopping channels will be co-opted by the entertainment channels, which will offer the same goods and services on their web sites and during their broadcasts. Viewers will not need to turn to the drama-less home shopping channels to make their online purchases.

CHAPTER FOUR

The Electronic Programming Guide: Don't Stay Home Without It

There is more to life than increasing its speed.
—*Mahatma Gandhi*

Gandhi never tried to use a TV guide to find something to watch. Of course, the great peace activist had things on his mind other than sifting through hundreds of pages of grids, rolling listings, VCR Plus codes, and episode descriptions. But if he thought bringing the British empire to its knees was a challenge, he should have tried finding out when episode #23 of *Star Trek* was playing in syndication. Now *that* would have been worthy of a Nobel Prize.

Indeed, the printed TV guide has become yet another American institution that has been beaten by time and technology. By sheer force and habit, the guide still stands today, but it is rapidly decaying at its foundation, and it's just a matter of time before it topples over. Of course, it was not always that way. In the so-called golden age of television—when there were just three channels—the weekly TV guide was as indispensable in the American household as the frozen dinner and freeze-dried coffee. And let me remove the small "g" from *guide* and upgrade it to a capital. I'm talking about *TV Guide*. The digest-size magazine was a beauty to behold—it covered the three networks like a blanket. Its program descriptions were so well done that it enticed you to tune in, and its feature stories were overflowing with juicy, behind-the-scenes reporting. And who can forget the lush covers of television's early icons, from Lucille Ball to James Arness? Well, it's not surprising that many avid TV watchers collected past editions of the magazine; it was as much a part of the television experience as the rabbit ears that sat atop the set.

However, the launch of cable TV in the 1980s, which added dozens of new channels to people's homes, eventually made *TV Guide* (and other guides) as attractive and user-friendly as the Manhattan white pages. The television guide had to dramatically increase the number of pages to include listings for the new channels. The desire to be complete was certainly a well-intentioned one—the guides were trying to please everyone—but it soon became nearly impossible to find what you were looking for. Information overkill began the slow death of the television guide.

Initially, *TV Guide* bucked the trend and ignored requests from readers and cable networks to include cable TV listings. The magazine's publishers believed that most readers spent 90 percent of their time watching CBS, NBC, or ABC. Therefore, the theory went, if they included cable listings, readers would cancel their subscriptions because the magazine would be too thick and hard to read. In addition, *TV Guide* was not enthusiastic about spending the money for the extra paper needed to add the cable channels. The concerns were justified, but *TV Guide* soon found its circulation starting to decline anyway, because consumers basically wanted it all; they wanted easy-to-read network listings and cable TV listings, a combination that was a financial and logistical impossibility. The printed edition of *TV Guide* never recovered from this "rock and a hard place" dilemma. The magazine's circulation, which once neared twenty million, had dipped to approximately twelve million by the year 2000.

The launch of the two-hundred-channel mini-satellite dish put another nail in the TV guide's coffin. If a magazine team couldn't successfully add fifty or sixty channels to their listings, how on earth were they going to handle two hundred? And what would happen when three hundred channels were available? Or five hundred? Or, God forbid, a thousand?

In 1994 when DIRECTV introduced the first eighteen-inch dish, I was the editor of a satellite TV guide called *Satellite DIRECT*. It was becoming increasingly clear to me that the blinding pace of technology was about to make my business a *Tyrannosaurus rex*. The future looked even bleaker when I got my first look at DIRECTV's Electronic Programming Guide (EPG). It was unlike anything I had ever seen. Cable TV's on-screen guide, which I had used before, was the least sophisticated example of technology since the invention of the hammer. It took what seemed to be a fortnight to scroll from the first channel to the last—and you couldn't interact with it, unless you call throwing a sofa pillow at the screen "interacting." You had to wait until the guide made its way to the channel listing you wanted to check out. But the satellite EPG, which popped up on your screen with the push of a button, let you click on a movie or show and instantly learn everything you needed to know and then some. The EPG stored detailed programming information for all two hundred channels. Shortly after the dish first hit the market, the EPG was updated to permit viewers to search for their favorite shows, actors, or genres. For instance, you could type in "John Wayne" and the EPG would immediately spit out the times, channels, and descriptions for every John Wayne film airing during the next seven days. After my first night of using the EPG, I remember going into work the next morning and telling my colleagues that we were in trouble. Of course, it was the equivalent of telling an alcoholic that the devil's hooch would eventually kill him; no one wanted to hear that the good times were coming to an end. But, heresy or not, it was clear to me that printed TV guides were living on borrowed time. (To its credit, the management team at *TV Guide* eventually acknowledged the hard truth and began to invest millions of dollars in developing its own EPG. More on that later.)

DIRECTV's EPG was an immediate success, particularly with younger viewers who were more comfortable with new technology. Many older viewers, who still had difficulty programming their VCRs, were a bit intimidated at first; consequently, we soon found that more than 50 percent of *Satellite DIRECT's* subscribers were over the age of fifty. This did not exactly endear us to the advertising community, which likes 'em young. As the years progressed, even older people started to get the hang of using the EPG, and our circulation began to plateau.

This period was the beginning of the end for the printed TV guide. And the ultimate demise is just ahead. Cable TV operators and most TV manufacturers are now including state-of-the-art EPGs in their new digital set-top boxes and TV sets. Nearly all Americans will soon have access to an on-screen guide that can:

- Permit you to search a week's worth of listings by actor, title, or genre.

- Remind you that one of your favorite shows is coming on, by flashing a message across the bottom of your screen.

- Permit you to record any show you want by clicking on its grid in the EPG. (The EPG can be connected either to a VCR or to a Personal Video Recorder. DIRECTV and The Dish Network, the two satellite TV operators, now offer receivers that have the PVR feature within the EPG itself; you can instruct your set-top box's hard drive to record a show by clicking on the programming grid. Cable TV will soon offer the same feature.)

- Guarantee you that your listings will be 100 percent accurate, because they are updated electronically every day. (Unlike the printed guide, which sometimes goes to press four to six weeks before the magazine is delivered to subscribers.)

- Permit you to customize your programming lineup so that only the channels you subscribe to, or only your favorites, appear in your grids.

In the face of such formidable competition, it is hard to envision a scenario where the traditional television guide can survive, particularly when you consider that the EPG is free while the printed TV guide requires a hefty annual subscription. It's the biggest mismatch since the Tyson-Spinks fight. This fact is not lost on the publishers of *TV Guide*. Anthea Disney, a former editor of *TV Guide* and a long-time employee of Rupert Murdoch's News Corp., was quoted in 1998 as saying that *TV Guide* would likely cut the listings from the magazine within five years. The reason: It couldn't possibly compete with the EPG. Embarrassed, News Corp., which then owned *TV Guide,* issued a press release saying Disney's comments were taken out of context. The company wanted to reassure advertisers who, after all, were still spending millions of dollars in that soon-to-be defunct listings magazine. However, many media observers believed that Disney had simply let the cat out of the bag. And just a year later, they seemed to be proven right when Gemstar purchased *TV Guide* for $9.2 billion. Gemstar, a high-tech company that manufactures the VCR Plus (see Chapter Two), does not exactly have a long history of publishing glossy, mass-circulation magazines. In a press conference announcing the sale, the company's owners promised to make *TV Guide* a leader in the field of Electronic Programming Guides. There was little talk about such issues as whether the magazine needed better writers or photographers.

Since the sale, Gemstar has struck agreements with TV manufacturers and cable TV operators to include a *TV Guide*–branded EPG in their sets and set-tops, respectively. *TV Guide*'s EPG will perform all of the usual EPG functions, plus give viewers an opportunity to interact with shows by voting on favorite performers and requesting more information. "We must establish credibility as a new medium . . . and we must get into as many devices as possible," says Henry Yuen, president and CEO of Gemstar.

Despite Gemstar's emphasis on the EPG, the printed *TV Guide* will not die overnight. As of this writing, it still has twelve million readers. But there's little doubt that its circulation will continue to shrink and that the guide—in fact, every television guide, including those in your daily paper—will have to undergo a series of dramatic changes. (See "Predictions.") It's hard not to be a little saddened by this. The EPG will make our lives more convenient and arguably more fun. But *TV Guide*'s print edition deserves much of the credit for the success of television itself. In the early days, television frightened many consumers; its stark, black-and-white broadcasts starring relative unknowns compared unfavorably with the warm, comforting voices of long-time radio personalities. But *TV Guide*'s weekly offering of colorful feature stories about new stars and shows made the medium seem exciting. It made people want to watch! *TV Guide*, as a corporate entity, will survive and perhaps even thrive in the EPG world. But *TV Guide*, the listings magazine that taught many people how to watch television, is on its last legs.

Predictions

■ **1.**

By the year 2004, the Electronic Programming Guide (EPG) will replace the printed TV guide as the primary way that viewers find out what's on television. The EPG will be an instant success for two reasons: (1) it will be free to all cable and satellite TV viewers, and (2) unlike the printed TV guide, which is published weeks in advance and therefore is dated by the time it reaches subscribers, the EPG will be updated every day via an electronic download. Consequently, the electronic guide will be 100 percent accurate—and it will allow viewers to search for their favorite actors and shows with the touch of a button. The EPG will be so dominant that it will be difficult to even find a TV listings guide at your local newsstand. *TV Guide,* which once had nearly twenty million subscribers, will dramatically scale down its print edition to concentrate on its own version of the EPG. Other publishers of paper TV guides will go out of business and/or sell their subscriber lists to *TV Guide* or another entertainment magazine.

■ **2.**

However, a handful of smart magazine publishers will shift gears and create a new kind of printed TV guide. The new publication will be overflowing with features, reviews, and behind-the-scenes stories about television—information that will not fit within the narrow grids of an EPG. The new TV guide will contain no listings—there will be no reason to include them, what with an EPG available on just about every television screen. However, the new publication *will* find an audience of people who are still interested in knowing more details about their favorite shows and stars and who prefer to read about them in a traditional print magazine rather than on a web site. Unlike an *Entertainment Weekly*, which covers everything from TV to movies to music, the new TV guide will focus exclusively on the world of television.

■ *3.*

Still, EPG companies will not let the new TV guides have the market to themselves. They eventually will insert web links into the grids that will take the viewer to a site giving more details on that program. For example, a listing for the movie *Eyes Wide Shut* would offer a link that would bring you to a Roger Ebert review of the film, or perhaps an interview with star Tom Cruise. In time, the EPG companies will go a bit further and actually provide a video of the Cruise interview. Click on *Eyes Wide Shut* in your EPG, and the Cruise interview will pop up in a window in the left-hand corner of the screen. Click on another icon in the *Eyes Wide Shut* grid, and the theatrical trailer for the film will appear.

■ *4.*

The competition to be the leading EPG will be as fierce as any in the ITV industry. EPG companies will spend millions of dollars lobbying cable and satellite TV operators to grant them the right to do their electronic guides. The reason: For many viewers, the EPG will be the first thing they look at when they turn on their television. The company that produces this "TV Home Page" will have a tremendous influence over what and when people watch. Consequently, a successful EPG will generate an incredible amount of advertising dollars from networks, studios, and just about every other company seeking to reach the TV audience.

5.

Companies will pay premium prices for small banner ads at the top of the EPG, but the real money will come from the insertion of small ads in the grids themselves. For example, a listing for the NBC show *Friends* could include a short message and web site link for Chevrolet underneath the program information. Most printed TV guides refuse to accept advertising in their grids because of fear that the reader would question the magazine's integrity. But the EPG companies will get away with it because the viewer will have been conditioned that e-commerce is an integral part of Interactive TV. The placement of an ad in an "editorial" space will seem perfectly normal. (By the way, if you are wondering how EPG companies are going to squeeze all this information into a programming grid, the Digital TV—the TV that will be coming to most viewers' homes during the next several years—will have a significantly larger screen. You will be able to display larger grids.)

6.

The EPG will offer many popular applications, but the "killer app" will be its capacity to record programs with the touch of a button. The EPG will be connected to the set-top box's Personal Video Recorder so that you will be able to search for a show in the grids and then instruct the PVR to record it. This feature will be so convenient and easy to use, viewers will keep coming back to the EPG to search for possible viewing choices. As we stated in prediction #4, the leading EPG companies will have unlimited influence because 100 percent of the audience will look at those guides every day—and sometimes several times a day.

7.

And even when you don't search the listings, the EPG will flash program reminders at the bottom of your screen based on your viewing preferences and history. For example, if you have watched four Cameron Diaz movies in the past month, the EPG might alert you that *Any Given Sunday* is playing on HBO tonight. The EPG will "know" to flash this reminder because it will have a record of every show you have watched—plus it will ask you for your viewing preferences when you sign up for your EPG service. Based on your record and your answers, the EPG will automatically remind you of shows that it "believes" you would enjoy.

8.

The EPG also will be able to forward program reminders to hand-held Net appliances, such as Palm Pilots. For example, you might turn on your Palm Pilot and find a message that says: "*Gone with the Wind* tonight on TBS." Hit a button on your Palm Pilot, and it will send an e-mail instructing your set-top box to record the movie.

■ **9.**

The EPG eventually will also offer a lineup of programming on the Web—a listing of the top celebrity chats and "shows." It's not hard to see, for example, that the EPG for Time Warner's cable TV systems would have a list of upcoming events on America Online. You would be able to drop in on those events by clicking on the grid; it would immediately connect you to AOL's Internet TV service.

CHAPTER FIVE

TV
dot
com

*I find that a great part of the information I have
was acquired by looking up something and finding
something else on the way.*
                              —Humorist Franklin P. Adams

Franklin P. Adams made his observation long before there
was a World Wide Web, but his words today could easily
describe what it's like to surf the Internet. The Web, which
has grown to more than fifty million pages in less than a
decade, is a virtual library filled with information on every
subject you could ever imagine. It's nearly impossible to
visit one web page without coming across something so interesting that it compels you to search another document or
an entirely different site. It's like eating that Lays potato
chip—you can't eat just one.

The Internet has also become the communications mode
of choice for many Americans, particularly younger people.

Once upon a time, a conversation between two friends ended with one of the parties saying, "Give me a call." Nowadays, the discussion is often closed with someone saying, "Send me an e-mail." In fact, some "relationships" consist almost entirely of e-mail messages and online "buddy" chats on America Online and other Internet services. You could certainly argue that this is not an improvement, but communicating by e-mail does give users greater control over their daily routine. Unlike the intrusive phone call, which must be dealt with that moment, e-mail correspondents decide when to read their messages and when to reply. Still, proponents of Charles Darwin could make a case that our increasing reliance on e-mail and other online written communications will eventually turn us into a race of distant, anonymous individuals, albeit tech-savvy and well-organized ones. The price of progress, huh?

The ability to buy and sell goods online is a less debatable attribute of the Net. E-commerce has been one of the great American success stories of the past century. The reason is simple: In most cases, it is far more efficient and sometimes less expensive to buy a product from a web site than it is to purchase it from a retail store. In addition, online customer service, despite its occasional burps, usually surpasses that of the retailer; anyone who has tried recently to get a sales clerk's attention can offer supporting evidence for that case.

The Revolution Has Just Begun

Yes, the Internet has changed the dynamic of everything from personal communications to business strategies to shopping habits. But despite suggestions in the media that the Net is pervasive in our society, many Americans rarely or never go online, particularly at home. Most studies indicate that less than 40 percent of Americans are "regular" users of the Internet—meaning they go online at least once a week. When the studies focus on home use, the number of "regular" users shrinks to less than one-third of the nation. The argument that America has become a tech-savvy, web-surfing nation is simply preposterous.

But what would happen if a larger percentage of the country became frequent users of the Internet? How influential would the medium be then? Well, we might find out for three reasons:

Faster Connections

Most Americans own a home PC that has a 33.6 or 56k modem. Consequently, they believe the Net is way too slow. And who can blame them? They are used to the instant gratification they get from watching television—when you change the channel, the next channel is there; you don't have to wait for it to download on your screen. (Can you imagine what that would be like? "Honey, that looks like George Clooney on the E! Channel. No, wait a minute, it's Ernest Borgnine!") The snail-like connections discourage many consumers from going online at all. However, cable TV companies are offering their subscribers an opportunity to upgrade those phone connections with high-speed, two-way cable lines that make surfing the Net like, well, like changing the channel. (The phone companies are offering a similar high-speed connection called a Digital Subscriber

Line, or DSL.) As of this writing, the cable TV companies are charging up to $40 a month for the privilege of owning a high-speed cable line. But cable will soon have a vested interest to lower the cost and make sure that most—if not all—cable subscribers will have a fast Internet connection.

Net TV

The vested interest? Cable companies are planning to add an Internet TV service to those spanking-new, digital set-top boxes. They know that more consumers will subscribe to the service if it comes with a high-speed line. The ramp-up may be slow—some cable operators may first add such features as Video on Demand and the Electronic Programming Guide—but eventually all cable subscribers will be offered an Internet TV service. In addition, DIRECTV, the largest satellite TV operator, is offering America Online along with its two-hundred-plus channels of programming. The Dish Network, DIRECTV's satellite rival, has a similar deal with Microsoft's WebTV. (Just so that we don't leave anyone out, U.S. West, the regional phone company, has launched a service called WebVision, which allows subscribers to access the Net on TV using a DSL line.)

Net TV will revolutionize the industry. The "lower class"—also known as residents of the Digital Divide—will be able to go online without having to buy a PC. Home PC owners who rarely go online because of concerns over reliability and speed will become frequent fliers when they start using TV's high-speed connection. And the person who doesn't like to surf at home because he doesn't want to break away from his television will suddenly have the Net on that television; he will be able to go on the Net and watch television at the same time. You start doing the math and you can envision a day when nearly all Americans are online—every day.

Before you run out and buy stock in Internet TV companies, I have to caution that the concept of surfing the Net on TV will seem a bit odd at first to most TV viewers. They don't have much practice in reading text on their screen, unless it's the batting average of a baseball player; wait until they try reading a lengthy news article about financial trends on a nineteen-inch screen. "Internet via the TV is totally different from the Internet people access through personal computers," says Jamison Ching, president of Set-Top.Com, a San Diego–based web site that provides links to web sites designed specifically for viewing on TV.

In addition, as noted above, many consumers are not familiar with the basics of going online, whether they are doing it on the TV or on a PC. For example, when I was the editor and publisher of *TV Online,* a magazine for WebTV users, I used to receive e-mails from readers who complained that they couldn't access a specific web site that had been mentioned in our publication. When I asked them why, I discovered that some people were trying to reach the site by typing its web address in the subject header of an e-mail and then sending it; they apparently thought the site would send back an e-mail that had its home page in the body of the letter. Other readers took to even more creative ways of trying to reach sites, ranging from badly misspelling the address to forgetting to put the "dot-com" at the end. The need for such precision left many WebTV owners questioning their decision to buy an Internet TV set-top box in the first place. Although the WebTV audience is not a perfect microcosm of the nation, it is fair to speculate that many consumers will have a similar experience when they first use their TVs to go online.

The Selling of Net TV

Consequently, Internet TV companies such as World Gate, America Online, and Microsoft's WebTV will spend billions of dollars to get people hooked on the new service—as well as to educate them about the benefits. "There is no other software business that is as dedicated to the vision of the TV . . . as we are," Microsoft Chairman and CEO Bill Gates told an industry conference in 1999. In addition to offering a high-speed connection, the Net TV firms will provide a variety of goodies, including:

On-Screen Chat Rooms: America Online is offering AOL-TV customers the ability to chat with other TV viewers while still watching their favorite show. For example, fans of the sci-fi hit *The X-Files* can exchange their thoughts on-screen while watching the action unfold. In addition, AOL is considering a feature that would inform a viewer that a friend is watching the same show she is. The viewer could then send a communication to her friend to ask her how she likes the program. The "Buddy Chat" feature is available on AOL's PC service, but the TV version could become an overnight sensation.

Video E-Mail: WebTV permits its customers to send still pictures and thirty-second audio bites along with their e-mail messages. However, WebTV and the other Net TV companies are expected to go one step further and allow consumers to send live-action, video e-mails. Instead of just jotting down some notes to your aunt in Idaho, you could send an actual video of yourself saying hi.

On-Screen Links to Web Sites: WorldGate, a Pennsylvania-based company that makes Net TV software for cable set-tops, has created what it calls "Hyper-Links," on-screen links that you can click on and go directly to web sites related to programming you are watching. WebTV offers a similar feature, but the web site link appears as an interactive icon (a lower-case I) in the right-hand corner of the screen. NBC and MSNBC have created interactive links for several of their news shows, including *The NBC Nightly News with Tom Brokaw* and *The News with Brian Williams*. The owner of a WebTV Plus set-top box can click on the icon and get more details on the day's top stories while still watching the program in a picture-within-a-picture window. The home viewer can also interact with the show by voting on news polls and chatting with other viewers about the news. NBC's interactive broadcast of Notre Dame football games, for example, permits fans to instantly retrieve up-to-the-minute stats on both teams' key players. Several other networks, including the Weather Channel, HBO, and PBS, are also creating interactive content for WebTV and other Net TV platforms.

"This product illustrates the future of Internet and television convergence," says John Nicol, general manager of MSNBC.com. "Interactive television components for NBC News will deliver content and services that create a more engaging, personalized experience, allowing viewers to interact with the broadcasts. The programming allows users to voice their opinions through online voting, chats, surveys and quizzes—during the actual broadcast."

Critics of the Net TV concept say the networks are wasting their time because the TV viewer is too "lazy" to interact with the programming. "The PC experience is interactive. You're clicking the mouse, entering information, moving stuff around," says Roger Black, who heads the Interactive Bureau, a web-site-design consulting firm. "TV is a laid-back, passive and sometimes even lying-down experience. Mixing the two seems unnatural." As you can imagine, these are fighting words to the folks who run the Net TV companies.

"Some Silicon Valley people think the PC is a much more sophisticated device than the TV, and that TV is an inferior platform for non-competent people," says Hal Krisbergh, WorldGate's CEO.

To be fair, I doubt that Roger Black believes that TV viewers are "non-competent." However, initial research of the WebTV audience—the nation's first community of Internet TV users—tends to support Krisbergh and his Net TV companions. It seems that once people start surfing the Net on TV, they can't get enough. A 1999 survey that I sponsored as editor and publisher of *TV Online* found that the average WebTV owner was online approximately fourteen hours a week, compared to twelve hours a week for the average PC owner. The more people who get Internet TV, the more likely it is that we will see what industry wonks like to call "a paradigm shift." "This shift will create a uniquely TV-centric, Internet-like experience in which the viewer's relation-

ship with the television will move from passive to interactive," says Leo J. Hindery, Jr., the former president and chief
executive officer of AT&T Broadband & Internet Services.
"Interactive television is entirely new and like nothing consumers have ever seen before."

Predictions

■ **1.**

The merger of the Internet and the TV will lead to a dramatic increase in the average number of hours that people are online. Millions of Americans who never or rarely
used the Net at home because it required firing up their
personal computers will find surfing from their couch to
be irresistibly easy. In addition, TV viewers will be more
likely to surf because there will be an "Internet" option on
their TV home page when they turn on their set; this
nightly reminder will serve as a psychological trigger that
will lead to greater use of the Net.

■ **2.**

The Internet TV service provided by cable and satellite
TV companies will include a high-speed, two-way con-
nection, through a cable modem, a Digital Subscriber Line
(DSL), or a satellite connection.

■ **3.**

Entertainment-related web sites, such as those for TV
shows, movies, and musical artists, will see an increase

in the number of hits to their sites. The reason: Surfers
will have entertainment on the mind because they will
be surfing with an entertainment appliance—the television—rather than with a work-related product—the PC.
Moreover, the networks will encourage viewers to go to
their web sites via messages before, during, and after
programs.

4.

Entertainment-related web sites will enhance their sites
with Video On Demand services and other features that
will either complement or compete with existing TV
channels. Thanks to advancements in broadband technology, scores of web sites will offer original programming
of a similar quality to what will be available on television.
The lines between a TV channel and a "TV web channel"
will blur.

5.

The average number of hours that people watch traditional television channels will decline slightly. However,
strong networks that build an equally strong Internet
presence will barely see a ripple in their ratings. Their web
sites—combined with shrewd, on-air promotion of the
sites—will increase brand awareness and viewer loyalty.
TV viewers, for example, may watch a show on NBC during which a message will encourage them to check out
NBC's web site for more information about that show.
While at the site, the viewer will get reminders about
other NBC shows airing later that night.

▪ **6.**

Consumers will begin to routinely use their television's picture-in-picture feature so that they can watch TV and surf the Net or check their e-mail at the same time. Smart network executives will develop programming that will enhance this practice; on-air messages will encourage consumers to open up a "window" on the screen that contains the show's web site.

▪ **7.**

The attention span of the TV viewer will shrink even further when viewers have the option to toggle back and forth from TV to the Net. Consequently, it will be more difficult for a network to keep an audience for a one-hour show, much less a two-hour one. The half-hour show, whether it's a sitcom or drama, will become the industry standard, despite initial resistance from the creative community.

▪ **8.**

Nightly network news programs will have to rely even more on pictures and exclusive features rather than showing talking heads merely reporting the daily news. The easy access to news web sites will make the Net TV viewer more informed about the news; the shows will refer them to sites for more details.

▪ **9.**

The web sites of network channels will become as important as the channels themselves. Networks will spend

millions to ensure that viewers find the sites as compelling as the programming. This will help reinforce
brand loyalty.

CHAPTER SIX

Niche TV

Nay, be a Columbus to whole new continents and worlds within you, opening new channels, not of trade, but of thought.

—Henry David Thoreau

One of the great myths of watching television is that it's often a solitary experience. The popular image of the TV viewer is that of the obsessed football fan or soap opera addict being glued to the tube, unable or unwilling to speak to another human being. Certainly, some TV shows are so absorbing that people tend to lose themselves in the plot and block out the idle chatter coming from family members in the living room. But after watching a particularly good show, the TV viewer is eager to share his thoughts with others. It's part of the experience. By talking with another person, the viewer can relive the positive emotions he or she felt during the show. It's also a great social device to bond with your fellow human beings. This explains why people gather around the water cooler and discuss a big game or special TV event the morning after its broadcast. Over the years, these impromptu "morning-afters" have been convened to discuss such historical TV moments as the last episodes of *Seinfeld, Cheers,* and *M*A*S*H;* the broadcast of the *Challenger* space shuttle explosion; the O.J. Simpson murder trial; and President Clinton's grand jury deposition about his affair with Monica Lewinsky. But most times, people have come together to simply chat about a funny moment in a favorite sitcom or perhaps some silly remark made by a network anchor during the evening news. Because we saw it on television, we saw it *together.*

But gathering around the water cooler to discuss a specific show is quickly becoming an antiquated practice. It's not because people suddenly think they don't have time for their coworkers (although in certain Silicon Valley offices a case could be made for that argument). The reason is that the increasing number of channels on cable and satellite TV has made it highly unlikely that a large number of workers watched the same show. During television's early days, when there were just three or four channels, the odds were good that a majority of your officemates or neighbors had tuned in the same show. For instance, in the early 1950s, the *Texaco Star Theatre* starring Milton Berle regularly captured more than 80 percent of the TV audience; that means that more than eight out of ten televisions that were turned on were turned on to a man who often dressed in women's clothing and was frequently hit in the face with a pie. Uncle Miltie's ratings had as much to do with the weak lineup running opposite him as his comic genius. Even in later years, when the networks invested more money in programming, hit shows like *All in the Family* and *Dallas* were watched by approximately 40 percent of the audience. The major three networks—CBS, NBC, and ABC—simply dominated the airwaves.

But since the launch of cable TV in the early 1980s, the networks' share of the audience has dropped like a rock. People might like to say that cable has "fifty-seven channels and nothing on," but they *are* watching. In the year 2000, all four networks combined (Fox being the fourth) are watched by approximately 40 percent of the audience. And the Myers Group, a New York research and consulting firm, says that by mid-decade eight networks will share 30 percent of the audience and the top four will get just two-thirds of that. If you walk into your office today and say, "Hey, did you see *Everybody Loves Raymond* last night on CBS?," it's not likely that many people, if any, will say yes—although the sitcom is one of the top-rated shows in the country. However, the viewing choices of your coworkers probably ran the gamut from an ESPN baseball game to an HBO movie to a History Channel documentary. When you have fifty-seven channels, you have fifty-seven chances that people are watching something different. How do you initiate a water cooler conversation about television based on those odds?

In 1994, the polarization of the television audience took a step further when DIRECTV introduced the eighteen-inch satellite dish, which featured more than two hundred channels, many of which did not even appear in most cable lineups. Dish owners often had little in common when discussing television shows with their friends and coworkers who subscribed to cable. For example, the DIRECTV owner might come into work on a Monday morning and talk about the NFL Sunday Ticket—an exclusive DIRECTV programming package that offers a live broadcast of every NFL game, every Sunday. The cable subscriber may have listened politely for a few minutes but eventually grew tired of hearing about something she couldn't watch. The conversation didn't just make it more difficult for two people to bond; one could argue that it might have led to an unspoken distance between the two. As a dish owner myself, I saw this scenario play itself out on more than a few occasions.

Polarization Leads to Pluralization

The final step in this evolution will come during the next few years when cable TV operators add dozens of new channels and other Interactive TV features to their digital set-top boxes. Both the cable and satellite TV subscriber will have daily access to hundreds of options, including a five-hundred-channel lineup, surfing the Net on TV, video on demand, and video games. (The Dish Network, a rival to DIRECTV's eighteen-inch dish, already sells a satellite system that provides five hundred channels as well as Net access and video games. DIRECTV is expected to follow suit in the near future, and the cable operators will not be far behind.) The multitude of choices will make the "water cooler chat" on TV-related topics virtually obsolete; it will be almost statistically impossible for even 5 percent of an office to have had the same TV experience from the night before. The exception to the rule will be when television airs a breaking news event or a special event such as the

Oscar broadcast, a big sporting event like the Super Bowl or the Olympics opening ceremonies, or the final episode of a popular program. In the last instance, though, you could envision most people using their Personal Video Recorder to record the show for later viewing. Many conversations will go like this: "Did you watch the final *E.R.* last night?" "No, I taped it. I'm going to watch it sometime over the weekend." End of conversation.

Most Americans will not even notice how Niche TV will change the social dynamic of the office or the neighborhood. Behavioral change is rarely recognized as it occurs; it's not as if people will sit around and wonder aloud why they don't discuss TV shows with groups of people any more. But there's a certain sadness in anticipating the day when this becomes the norm. For better or worse, we are a generation that was raised and weaned on television—in fact, many people say their first memories were of TV shows. Perhaps as much as anything in our culture, television has acted as a catalyst to initiate social exchange. But the rules are changing. Americans will continue to discuss the television experience, but the conversations will be more exclusive; a viewer will seek out someone who she knows has a similar favorite channel or TV activity, rather than opening up a dialogue with a group. For example, a fan of the History Channel will initiate a discussion about a previous night's documentary with a fellow history buff. A video game enthusiast will talk about *Doom* with another game player. The cultural phenomenon of reliving a TV experience by discussing it with a fellow human being will go on, but the circle of discussion will definitely get smaller.

New Channels

People will be quite happy, though, to trade any social disruption for the sudden availability of hundreds of channels. Nielsen research sponsored by *Satellite DIRECT* magazine, of which I used to be publisher, found that the number one reason that people purchased a satellite dish in the 1990s was "variety of channels." DIRECTV executives used to boast of satellite TV's crisp picture and CD-quality sound, but the real lure was that it had three times more channels than cable. TV viewers want more options, and both cable and satellite are going to deliver.

Many new channel slots will be devoted to pay-per-view and video on demand services, because they generate revenue in addition to basic and premium programming packages. However, the law of diminishing returns suggests that you can't fill out a five-hundred-channel lineup with just pay-as-you-go movies and events. Cable and satellite TV operators will have to add a large number of niche channels designed to appeal to special interests. (See "Predictions.") DIRECTV, whose two-hundred-channel lineup once featured approximately sixty PPV channels, learned that lesson the hard way; its customers wanted more "real" channels, and they were not shy about letting the satellite operator know. In later years, DIRECTV cut back on its PPV lineup and added more niche channels.

Because of satellite TV—and in anticipation of a five-hundred-channel digital cable lineup—dozens of niche channels launched in the late 1990s; several channels, such as the Golf Channel, ZDTV, and the Food Network, became overnight successes. The niche channel found that it only had to demonstrate that it could deliver a loyal audience to attract advertising dollars. The audience didn't even need to be a large one; in fact, for some advertisers, it was just as well that it was not. The advertisers wanted to reach people who were zealous about a particular subject, because they were more likely to buy products in that category. The concept of "target advertising" was the buzz on Madison Avenue.

"How much would an advertiser pay for an audience of two, for one hour, if that two happened to be Bill Gates and Warren Buffett?" David Neuman, president of the Digital Entertainment Network (DEN), asked at a 1999 industry conference.

Neuman was having fun with the concept, but his words were well taken. Television is no longer the exclusive playground of the big four networks; anyone who can deliver a desirable niche audience can make money. And it doesn't even have to be a "TV channel." In the world of digital TV, viewers will be able to surf over to the Net and find special interest programming there. Icebox.com is one of many web sites that offer "streaming video" of short films and programs. Broadcast.com provides live and recorded broadcasts of local radio and TV programming from across the nation. For instance, you can log on to Broadcast.com and watch a live broadcast of the local evening news on ABC's affiliate in New York.

"When we first started broadcasting Net radio, people said, 'Who's going to turn a four-thousand-dollar PC into a six-dollar radio?,' but then Net radio really took off," says Mark Cuban, cofounder of Broadcast.com. "People found they could get programming they couldn't get any other way. It's the same with Net video. Who thought people would take to satellite TV, to having to climb up on a roof and actually install a dish? This is something that could come easily into your home and offer you programming you choose, any time you like. How can that not succeed?"

Some say that Niche TV—whether it's on the Net or TV itself—will quickly end the domination of the big four networks. "The attack of technology is going to overrun TV, and the boneheads who run the networks are trying to figure out how to defend themselves," Gary Arlen, president of Arlen Communications, told *Red Herring* magazine in 1999.

But as we noted in other chapters, the networks are adapting to the new technology, albeit slowly. They have invested millions of dollars in Personal Video Recorder technology, developed content for Interactive TV programs, and, in some cases, launched niche channels of their own. NBC, for instance, also owns the news channel MSNBC and the business channel CNBC. The networks will never return to the days when a single show could capture more than 80 percent of the TV viewing audience. But they *will* remain powerful and pervasive.

Predictions

▪ *1.*

Digital TV will allow cable and satellite TV companies to offer hundreds of channels. Many of the additional channels will be devoted to pay-per-view and Video On Demand (VOD) services, which generate ancillary income for the operators. However, channels for audiences as narrow as Civil War buffs or wrestling fanatics will find a place on Digital TV because they will be able to capture enough viewers to sell advertising. Advertisers will seek out marketing partnerships with niche channels, for the niche audience will be particularly loyal to the channel's subject matter. Consequently, niche viewers will be more likely to buy products related to the channel and its genre.

▪ **2.**

Some likely new channels that will launch in the next several years:

- ▪ The Business Traveler Channel: It would appeal to the growing number of people who spend half of their lives on the road.

- ▪ The Pro Wrestling Channel: The sport had a tremendous resurgence in the late 1990s and continues to demonstrate that it can capture a loyal if slightly insane audience.

- ▪ The Welcome Wagon Channel: More than 40 million Americans move every year. A twenty-four-hour channel that offered tips on how to cope with the move and assimilate in a new city could be an instant hit.

- ▪ The Future Channel: The explosion of new high-tech products and services has created a strong curiosity about the future. Consumers, particularly those who have investments in Internet stocks, have become keenly aware that new inventions could have a significant impact on their pocketbooks.

■ *3.*

Niche TV will lead to a more fragmented audience and pluralist society. The days when coworkers gathered around the water cooler to discuss a specific TV show will come to an end, because no one show will capture a large percentage of the audience. Instead, people will seek out those who have similar interests and will discuss web sites and TV channels targeted to that interest.

■ *4.*

The proliferation of channels and the continued short attention span of viewers will dramatically change the dynamic and importance of the Nielsen ratings. The producer of a top-rated network show will be happy if he can capture 10 percent of the potential viewing audience, compared to the 23 to 30 percent share enjoyed by ABC's top-rated *Who Wants to Be a Millionaire*. On any given night, the audience will be spread over hundreds of channels, web sites, and PVR backlogs of previously recorded shows. "We, as consumers, used to receive our messages about brands in this great mass medium called television," Susan Ellis, executive vice president at the advertising agency BBDO, told the *Philadelphia Inquirer*. "It was the great cultural collector. That isn't true anymore. We have fragmented as a country and it [TV] has fragmented as a medium."

■ *5.*

The viewer's short attention span could soon lead to multi-channel viewing. With a large-screen digital TV, viewers of the future will likely be able to watch four or five channels at the same time—all displayed in windows on screen. Another window will likely display a web site or perhaps the family's e-mail list. The TV of tomorrow will start to look like the PC of today.

6.

The networks will continue to launch new niche services in an effort to retain viewers—even if those viewers are scattered over a number of channels. (The trend began in the 1990s when NBC launched MSNBC and CNBC.) Tomorrow's TV watchers will have an even shorter attention span than today's viewers. A network will need several channels that appeal to different interests, to have any hope of capturing the wandering channel surfer.

7.

Networks will also continue the trend of placing their shows on "partner" channels after the show's initial viewing. NBC, for example, has aired *Law and Order: Special Victims Unit* on the USA Network after it first aired on the peacock network. The idea is to make sure your program finds an audience, no matter where they flip to. Likewise, the show could be included on the network's web site for downloading, just in case some viewers forgot to set their Personal Video Recorder.

8.

The increase in pay-per-view channels and Video On Demand services will contribute greatly to creating a splintered audience. It will be more difficult to generate a sizable au-

dience for any given program, because a large percentage of
viewers will be watching movies or specials on PPV or VOD.

9.

The ability to provide more channels will put pressure on
the networks as well as cable and satellite operators to find
new content. There will be a hot market for young filmmakers and writers who can create programming that will
fill vast amounts of air time and sell advertising to pay for it.

10.

The ability to surf the Net on TV will prompt Internet
companies to create special-interest video channels on
their web sites. With improvements in broadband technology, the viewer will soon see little difference between
the quality of a video channel on TV and a video channel
on the Net. This will lead to a blur of the differences between TV and the Net.

11.

Using the Personal Video Recorder, viewers will develop
their own niche channels. For example, by instructing the
PVR to record any program that has "sewing" in its title
or description, a viewer will be able to create "The Sewing
Channel"—an inventory of shows related to sewing.
Then, when the viewer is ready, he will watch his cus-
tomized lineup of shows.

CHAPTER SEVEN

How Did a Video Store Get into My TV?

There is no place more delightful than home.
—Marcus Tullius Cicero

In the late 1970s, the center of my universe was located in a parking lot of a large shopping mall a few miles from my home in suburban Washington, D.C. It was there that a small, white shack of a store called Fotomat sat forlornly, all by itself. I visited Fotomat two or three times a week—not because I felt sorry for the poor clerk who was testing the limits of claustrophobia inside that little white hut. It wasn't even because of its one-hour photo service. It was because Fotomat had launched a service that would change my life and the lives of all movie fans. The photo development chain had started to rent videotapes of new and old films at ten dollars a pop. Fotomat was not the first store in the nation to offer this service; in fact, a handful of video rental stores were scattered about the Washington, D.C., area. But

Fotomat brought convenience and reliability to the video rental business. Since there was a Fotomat in just about every neighborhood, you didn't have to drive all over town to rent a movie.

I realize that I am dating myself in my enthusiastic recollection of this time. Renting a movie has long been taken for granted in our culture; today, video rental stores are outnumbered only by corner coffee shops. But some two decades ago it was remarkable that you could bring home a movie and watch it that night in the comfort of your living room. This was a luxury previously reserved for First Families, movie directors, and chaps who wore ascots and berets. In fact, it was such a novelty—and convenience— that I found myself renting films that I otherwise would never want to see. I also was more inclined to give a positive review to a movie I watched at home. In fact, I recall comparing Burt favorably to Bergman after sitting through my second viewing of *Smokey and the Bandit.* (Over the years, the lower standard of the home video consumer has become legendary. How many times have you seen people rent a video they've never heard of because they were tired of looking through blocks of shelves, the latest releases were snapped up, or they just wanted to get out of the store?)

Fotomat stayed in the video business about as long as it took it to develop a roll of negatives. In retrospect, that appears to be one of the great business blunders of all time. But don't you think the addition of a videotape library made things a bit crowded in that little booth? First things first, you know. Fortunately, Blockbuster and other video rental chains emerged to meet the demand of the growing audience of VCR owners.

The video rental business had an immediate and dramatic impact on our culture and the entertainment industry. For example:

- Phrases such as "I'll wait until it comes out on video"—meaning the film wasn't worth spending the bucks to see it in the theater—became part of our language.

- Many families started spending their nights at home snuggled up watching videos rather than going out in search of entertainment. The convenience of watching a movie at home (and the launch of the multi-channel cable TV lineup) contributed to the "cocooning" trend of the 1980s and 1990s.

- In the 1980s, the studios, under pressure from theater owners for movies that could compete with video and cable TV, increased their production of big-budget, special effects–laden films. The theory was that consumers needed something spectacular to get them out of the house. The plot became less important than the explosions or the fifty creative ways you could slice-and-dice the bad guys. This trend lasted for the next twenty years as directors and producers tried to top themselves with bigger and bigger spectacles. (Interestingly, the 1970s, the decade before the explosion of home video, featured some of the best films in history, and they were all

driven by strong characters and stories: *The Godfa-
ther, Chinatown, Rocky, Network, The Deer Hunter,* and
Taxi Driver. The film that most critics regard as Mar-
tin Scorsese's best work, *Raging Bull,* was also made
in the 1970s, although it was released in 1980.)

Pay Per View

Originality in the American entertainment industry is as rare
as a bicyclist who obeys traffic laws. The prevailing wisdom
is that it's downright silly to create a new product when you
can borrow from the fruits of another. Consequently, in the
late 1980s and into the '90s, cable TV operators tried to copy
the success of home video by adding a handful of pay-per-
view movie channels to their lineup. The effort was met with
total indifference because cable TV and their studio partners
failed to understand the fundamental reasons behind the
success of the video rental business: convenience and control. The video customer decided when to watch the video.
In fact, she could pause the film in the middle and watch the
rest of it later. However, to watch a pay-per-view film, the
cable TV viewer had to call an operator and request the
movie—and then wait up to two hours for it to begin. And,
in contrast to the endless volume of films at the local video
store, the pay-per-view customer could only select from
three or four movies. The PPV business was such a dog that
even using the phrase "pay-per-view" in marketing promo-
tions was considered to be a no-no because it had such a
negative connotation. The prevailing wisdom was that consumers would never pay a fee to order a movie at home.

Just when PPV appeared in need of a proper funeral, a company created by a bunch of (literal) rocket scientists and automakers gave it new life. In 1994, DIRECTV, which was owned by Hughes Electronics, which in turned was owned by General Motors, introduced the eighteen-inch satellite dish. The dish, the first legitimate alternative to cable TV, featured nearly two-hundred channels, including five different versions of HBO and both East Coast and West Coast feeds for several basic cable networks. But the match that lit the fuse, as rocket scientists like to say, was that DIRECTV devoted sixty channels to pay-per-view movies. DIRECTV's critics—namely people involved in protecting the cable TV business from well-heeled competitors—said they didn't understand the needs of the average TV viewer. They suggested that the Hughes/General Motors team might want to go back to booster rockets and Cadillacs.

But DIRECTV believed that consumers would flip for pay-per-view if it could be made as convenient as renting videos. In fact, DIRECTV went one step better and made it *more* convenient. With sixty PPV channels, DIRECTV's customers could choose from up to seventy different films a day. It wasn't quite the selection of a video store, but it certainly sufficed. More important, viewers could order a film with their remote control—and the movie cost just $2.99, a buck less than on cable TV. And, finally, some hit films aired every thirty minutes, the closest thing to "Video On Demand" that anyone had ever seen.

DIRECTV's pay-per-view offering was an overnight sensation. Dish owners ordered an average of two to three movies a month—seven times the rate that cable TV viewers ordered PPV. As publisher of *Satellite DIRECT* magazine, which reported on the small dish industry, I commissioned a Nielsen Media Research study of pay-per-view buying habits. We found that a majority of dish owners had stopped going to the video store; they said the lineup of PPV films was like having a video store in their TV. The magazine later published an article on this phenomenon entitled "Bye, Bye, Blockbuster?"—a suggestion that the video rental store could soon be extinct.

As you can imagine, the home video industry—Blockbuster Video in particular—reacted as if war had been declared. They demanded that the studios increase the "pay-per-view window"—the number of days a satellite or cable TV company could air a film after it was released on video. Some studio pay-television divisions had set DIRECTV's window at thirty days as a reward for devoting so many channels to PPV. (Video came first in the pecking order because the industry was generating billions of dollars in sales, while satellite's PPV business was still in its infancy.) But with a thirty-day window, the video rental companies—and the turf-protecting home video divisions of the studios—charged that satellite TV viewers were content to wait for the PPV premiere. Of course, they were right, although the intellectual force of their argument was not the deciding factor; it rarely is in Hollywood. Home video was the cash cow, while PPV was just a promising heifer; the studios expanded the window to a minimum of forty-five days. Satellite's PPV sales slowed a bit after that, although its growth rate still far surpassed that of cable TV.

The video industry's assault on pay-per-view was amusing when put in historical perspective. In the previous decade, theater owners had waged the same campaign against the rapidly growing video rental business; they argued for longer windows in between the time a film played in the theater and when it was released on video. The home video industry cried foul; what comes around, goes around.

But as philosopher George Santayana once said, "Fanaticism consists of redoubling your effort when you have forgotten your aim." The video industry's zealous, almost self-righteous attack on PPV was a clear demonstration that it had forgotten its aim. The video rental business was born to offer consumers a convenient and inexpensive way to watch movies at home. The pay-per-view business was simply doing that a little bit better.

Video On Demand

But the video industry finally woke up one morning and saw the technology written on the wall. Blockbuster Video announced in 1999 that it was entering the Video On Demand/Pay-Per-View business. The retailing giant said it planned to offer consumers the opportunity to rent videos from home by downloading them from their web site, Blockbuster.com. Using a digital set-top box that included a broadband Internet TV service, the TV viewer would call up Blockbuster.com, would click on a favorite movie, and the site would then electronically transmit the film to his set-top's hard disk drive. The viewer could then watch the film anytime he desired. (This will not occur until cable and satellite TV companies roll out those broadband Internet TV services, but that is expected to happen during the next few years. Forrester Research estimates that 27 million homes will have broadband Internet by the year 2003.) In addition, Blockbuster struck an agreement with Personal Video Recorder company TiVo that will permit TiVo customers to order a video from an on-screen lineup of films. The viewer would just have to click on the title, and the film would immediately begin playing.

"This announcement is an exciting step for Blockbuster as we continue to pursue avenues for our customers to receive quality in-house entertainment through electronic delivery," said Shellye Archambeau, president of Blockbuster.com, the video retailer's web site.

Blockbuster, of course, is not the first company to launch a Video On Demand business. But the retailer will help drive an industry that most experts believe will revolutionize the concept of watching movies at home. And with a digital set-top box that has a capacity for hundreds of channels, cable and satellite TV companies will offer scores of PPV channels and Video On Demand services. For example, the Intertainer, a Los Angeles–based company that is targeting the digital cable market, plans to offer six hundred hours a week of VOD programming, including feature films on PPV, for $3.95 per film. "We believe that high-quality programming is crucial. We're trying to build a deep library of first-run content. People want a lot of content," says Jonathan Taplin, copartner of the Intertainer and a former Hollywood producer of such films as *Mean Streets.*

Predictions

▪ *1.*

American consumers who want more control over their viewing schedules will instantly embrace Video On Demand and pay-per-view services. The average viewer will order a minimum of three VOD/PPV movies a month—and the number will increase when video retail companies such as Blockbuster begin offering consumers the ability to download videos from a large lineup.

▪ *2.*

Bye, bye, Blockbuster? Well, the brick-and-mortar video store will become a thing of the past. But Blockbuster and other video companies will set up online VOD/PPV stores that permit customers to download their favorite videos. The convenience of "renting" videos electronically will initially lead to a boom for Blockbuster and other online video rental businesses. Blockbuster, which many analysts have said will not survive the new digital world, could instead become the Amazon.com of the video industry.

▪ *3.*

The massive lineup of films on VOD, PPV, and Blockbuster online will put great pressure on subscription movie channels, such as HBO, to develop new ways to retain and attract customers. After all, the consumer can only watch so many films. Look for HBO and Showtime to cut back on their theatrical movie lineups and invest even more money on original programming such as *The Sopranos,* live con-

certs, and live sporting events such as boxing. In fact, it
would not be surprising to see HBO get into the high-
dollar competition for the rights to broadcast National
Football League and Major League Baseball games.

4.

Despite the growth of VOD services, sales of DVD players will continue to soar in the next few years because of
the format's exceptional picture quality and its capacity to
provide supplemental material such as "director's cuts"
and filmmaker commentaries.

5.

In time, however, the DVD will struggle because VOD
services will eventually match the DVD in both picture
quality and extra content. In addition, the VOD service
will have a spot in the digital cable and satellite TV programming lineups, making it easy for a consumer to purchase a VOD movie. The DVD, however, would have to
be ordered separately. Consequently, the convenience of
VOD will eventually lead to consumers stacking their
DVD boxes atop their old VCRs: in the closet.

6.

Network web sites will begin to offer catalogs of their past
TV shows, which can be ordered and downloaded in seconds to a consumer's set-top box. For example, a viewer
could call up a 1963 *Tonight* show starring Johnny Car-
son, a video of the fourth game of the 1968 World Series,
or any other show that's been preserved over the years.

The recent success of such nostalgia channels as TV Land and Classic Sports Network has proven that there is a strong market for visiting TV's golden years. The networks may be confounded to find, in a future world, that their greatest profits will come from their past.

7.

Impressed by the newfound success of PPV, the movie studios will experiment with putting first-run films on PPV. For example, the new Tom Cruise summer film could be made available to PPV viewers on a one-night-only basis—but on the same day as the film's premiere in movie theaters. The studios would charge a higher price than the ticket to the movie theater. The reason: to see if consumers will pay a premium price to see a new film in the comfort of their own home rather than having to stand in line at the theater and perhaps being bothered by a loquacious teenager in the next row. The experiment will be controversial in the film world. Theater owners will scream bloody murder, much as they did when the studios decided to support the fledgling video industry in the 1980s. But the studios will take the gamble, because of PPV's tremendous potential—as well as a lingering belief that many older consumers wait for a new film to premiere on PPV or a subscription movie channel.

8.

The growth of PPV will unquestionably put a strain on the local movie theater. The launch of a Blockbuster online could even be a telling blow for many theater owners struggling for audiences. The movie theater and the video store have been in a fair fight during the last two decades—both require consumers to leave their homes, brave the elements, and mix with strangers. When a consumer is thinking about watching a film, the major difference between going to the theater and the video store is the amount of time the consumer's family will be away from home. However, the store's ability to deliver a movie electronically to a consumer's set-top box will give the video rental business a huge advantage. The consumer will not have to leave his couch to "pick up" the latest top rental. To counter this edge, theaters will have to take a number of steps to compel the consumer to leave the house, including upgrading their sound systems, seating areas, and concession stands. The movie theater experience will have to become a special one, much as it was in the 1930s and '40s before the advent of television; people actually dressed up in their Sunday best to see a film! Theater owners will have to make their theaters fun, entertaining places to be, from the moment consumers walk into the door to the moment they leave.

9.

Another problem for the theater owner? The "home theater" trend—consumers building mini movie-theaters in their living or rec rooms—will continue to accelerate. Many viewers will want a big screen TV and a great sound system to take maximum advantage of the new interactive features, particularly PPV and VOD. The theater owner will have to compete with a family room that approximates the movie theater experience.

■ *10.*

The networks will also experiment with offering special broadcasts on PPV. The memory of NBC's failure with the Olympics on PPV in the 1990s is still fresh in the minds of many network executives. Consumers clearly had no interest in paying for a broadcast that they expected to be "free." But the growth of PPV and VOD over the next several years will change consumers' attitudes toward the format. Viewers will be more willing to pay for what once was considered "free."

CHAPTER EIGHT

You've Got a Phone Call... on Your TV?

What is it you want? Vast forces dormant in nuggets of imprisoned sunlight? Machines that fly, think, transport, fashion and do man's work? Images divine and graven? The products of philosophy, which is the guide of life, and knowledge, which is power? We have them all.
—Robert Moses, president of the 1964–1965 World's Fair in New York

The telephone is the greatest nuisance among conveniences; the greatest convenience among nuisances.
—Sociologist Robert Staughton Lynd

The "Picture Phone" was one of the star attractions of the 1964–1965 World's Fair in New York, along with Michelangelo's *Pieta*, a 360-degree movie screen, and a computer that would help you choose an appropriate hair color. Fairgoers

lined up for hours for an opportunity to sit down in front
of a small TV screen so that they could talk to another person who was sitting down in front of another small TV
screen. Even First Lady "Ladybird" Johnson, taking a break
from her campaign to beautify the nation, stopped by to
give it a try. Fortunately for marital bliss, President Johnson,
who was known to have a wandering eye, was not on the
other end of the line.

The fact that the people on the other end of the line were
actually tourists at a similar exhibit at Disneyland, on the
opposite coast, was hardly relevant. Sure, under normal cir-
cumstances, you would not wait for hours to talk by phone
with a person from Des Moines who had a stuffed Mickey
Mouse in one hand and a Pepsi in the other. But this was
the Space Age, a time when our presidents said we would
go to the moon by the end of the decade and when liquid
drinks could be stored in a bottle of dust called Tang. Did
common sense really matter? No. It was a time to explore
what we *could* do—not necessarily what we *needed* to do.

During the Fair, futurists predicted that the video phone
would be in every American home by the end of the century. Publisher Hugh Hefner was so taken with the idea that
he immediately installed Picture Phones at the famous Playboy mansion. Compiling a list of the possible ways that Hef
availed himself of the Picture Phone would require a meeting of the minds between Dr. Ruth Westheimer and
Olympian gymnastic coach Bela Karolyi. But that's OK.
Most advocates of the video phone were contemplating that
it would have more conventional applications anyway.
Why, you could watch our boys walk on the Moon and then

call your Aunt Edna who lived two thousand miles away and have a video chat about the historic event. The sheer thought of such Buck Rogers brilliance made many Americans giddy with excitement, although the effect could have been caused in part by the consumption of a cold glass of Tang. Ma Bell—the nation's phone company before the federal judicial system got into the long distance business—estimated that the video phone would generate billions of dollars in revenue in the next ten to twenty years.

However, present company excepted, the futurists often get it wrong. Just as Tang moved further back in your parents' cupboard until it was finally behind the Aunt Jemima pancake syrup and the Calumet Baking Powder, which featured an Apache warrior on the can (weren't the 1960s truly the Era of Enlightenment?), the video phone moved further back in our collective subconscious. In 1970, Ma Bell spent nearly a billion dollars on a marketing campaign to persuade Americans to put a Picture Phone in their homes. But the phone company found that consumer demand was weaker than a cup of Maxwell House and that the technology involved in delivering a consumer-friendly video phone to every home was on a par with the Apollo project. The phone worked just fine, but the video was space age indeed—the person on the other end of the line looked like she was on another planet. It also didn't help that Ma Bell set the monthly subscription fee at $125; no one could see the logic of that, even with a video phone.

The general lack of interest among consumers really shouldn't have come as any great surprise to the folks at Ma Bell. The average American family in 1970 was not ready for prime time. Most couples were struggling to keep up with the Joneses while simultaneously keeping an eye on the growing brood that was a by-product of the post–World War II years. The living room looked more like a demilitarized zone than a TV studio. Stacks of *Life* and *Look* piled up on the coffee table, spilling over onto the shag carpet; kids ran screaming from room to room, settling down only for thirty minutes or so to watch a favorite TV show. Teenagers, emboldened by television images of protests in the streets over the Vietnam War, became rebels with a cause—and they caused their parents a lot of grief. Who wanted this scene displayed on a video phone for all the world to see?

"A Picture Phone added little to phone conversations and sometimes even got in the way," Dr. A. Michael Noll, a former AT&T official involved in the development of the video phone, told *Retro Future,* a webzine. "The acoustical intimacy of a phone call was shattered by the visual imagery."

No, Americans wanted to seal their anonymity when they entered their squared castles. They certainly were happy to take phone calls—what a great way to share your misery with others!—but they didn't want the other person to *see* them. What if they weren't dressed? Or their hair was out of place?

The Picture Phone became a relic before it ever became a reality. Ma Bell put it on the shelf along with five-digit phone numbers.

Back to the Future

But more than three decades later, we again find ourselves in an age that encourages people to explore what can be done and finding out later if anyone wants to do it. Several leading communications companies, including Intel, AT&T, and Sega, are talking about bringing the video phone back to the future. Intel, in fact, has already introduced the Intel Video Phone, which enables PC users to have video conversations over the Net. And in early 2000, Sega launched the Dreameye, a small digital video camera that sits atop your TV and allows you to send video e-mail and have TV phone chats. The viewer wears a headset to talk to the person on the other line. (Like Dreamcast, Sega's Internet-based game player, the Dreameye was first introduced in Japan but is expected to soon make its way to the United States.) "Sega is committed to providing people with the power to do more with the Dreamcast system," said Hideki Sato, corporate senior vice president at Sega Enterprises. "We want people to have more fun with the network, be more creative and communicate with more people."

C. Michael Armstrong, the chairman of AT&T, envisions a living room of the future where all activity flows from the tube. Whether it's Hollywood entertainment, the Internet, video games, or telephone calls, you'll do it on your TV. "Technology is erasing the boundaries of televisions, telephones and computers," Armstrong said in a keynote address to the October 1999 Internet World conference. "The cable box on your TV will not only let you order all the PPV movies you want, but it will be a virtual communications center."

True, the "Broadcasting Live from Mars" quality of today's video phones leaves something to be desired, but improvements in digital technology will change that. Broadband Internet TV, which will be included in cable and satellite TV

set-top boxes over the next few years, will soon make the
TV phone call as easy as clicking on your remote when the
phone rings or, as I should say, when the TV rings.

Before you click your tongue and smugly say, "There they
go again," take into consideration that much has changed
since 1970 when Ma Bell's Picture Phone faded to black:

- With the introduction of cable and satellite TV systems, cell phones, and handheld electronic organiz-
  ers, Americans have become more open minded
  about new technology. In fact, in a new twist on the
  old practice of keeping up with the Joneses, many
  people (particularly Type A males) will buy the latest
  gadget because it's cool to do so. I've seen grown men
  taking out their cell phones, pagers, and Palm Pilots
  and showing them around as if they were pictures of
  their kids. I've also seen those same people confess
  that they are not entirely sure how to use their new
  acquisitions. "Buy the toy first; discover its application later"—that's become the motto for many.

- In the last several years, millions of Americans have
  plopped little digital cameras atop their personal
  computers so that they can have video chats with
  fellow Net surfers around the country. The idea
  that someone can see you while you're talking on
  the phone appears to be less frightening than it
  used to be.

- Thanks to digital technology, tomorrow's video
  phone will provide crisp pictures and sound—in

great contrast to the Picture Phone and even today's "webcams." Aunt Edna won't look like she's underwater when you call to chat.

- New advances such as caller I.D. and call waiting have changed our concept of what a telephone can do. In 1970, the phone could do only one thing— enable you to talk to another person. But today's phones are mini-computers filled with all kinds of programs and features. For example, The Dish Network, a satellite TV company, offers its customers an on-screen caller I.D. When someone calls you, that person's telephone number will appear on your TV screen. In today's environment, a video phone suddenly doesn't seem out of the ordinary.

- In the year 2000, approximately 15 million Americans were working from home, and studies indicate that millions more wanted to do the same. They would probably get that chance if the boss could touch base with them via a video phone. Consequently, this time, the phone company might get a different answer when they ask if consumers want a phone with a screen.

"Person-to-person image communication will be the killer application for broadband Internet in the same way that text has been for the Internet and that speech was for the telephone," says Fred Kappetijn, who heads Ex'ovision, a California-based company that is developing video phones for the Net.

Still, let's not overlook the basic inconsistent nature of the human being, particularly the American human being. For the reasons stated above, the video phone is an idea that seems right for the time. But Americans were in love with the concept back in 1964. What will happen when people realize that someone could invade their privacy at any given moment? Will they feel comfortable enough with their appearance that they will be prepared to answer the video phone every hour of the day? And if not, then what? Will they stop taking video phone calls? Will they sometimes turn the video off and insist on having an audio-only conversation? How would that affect the relationship between the two people on the phone, particularly if one person demands a video call? Clearly, there are a few issues that need to be worked out. But some critics say that the video phone is simply a bad idea—then *and* now.

"Flops and failures are not always allowed to rest in peace. Why should the video phone succeed now?" asks Michael Noll, the former AT&T official.

Predictions

■ *1.*

Most Americans will initially resist the video phone because of their concern that callers will see them in, shall we say, less than flattering moments. Consequently, the phone companies will have to invest in an extensive education and marketing campaign to promote the benefits of video phone calls. In time, more and more people will embrace the concept as a way to talk to—and see—friends and loved ones who live in another state. Still, in the early stages of the video phone and perhaps well after that, callers will have disagreements over whether the video should be "turned on" or not. (The video phone will have to give consumers the option.) Some consumers will prefer to have an audio-only conversation, while others will push for both parties to be able to see each other. It's not hard to predict that this running debate will be satirized in phone company commercials designed to make consumers more comfortable with the video phone. BOYFRIEND: "Turn it on!" GIRLFRIEND: "No, my hair is a mess!" BOYFRIEND: "I don't care about your hair. I want to see you!" GIRLFRIEND: "Not like this, you don't!" CUE THE NARRATOR: "The Video Phone: Turn It On When You Want to Be Turned On." THE NEXT SCENE: The girlfriend has just come back from the hair salon and she has called her boyfriend. This time, she hits the Video button. BOYFRIEND: "Wow!" GIRLFRIEND: "Why are you wearing that sweater again? I told you not to wear that sweater..." FADE TO BLACK.

■ 2.

There's no substitute for being able to see someone when you are talking to her. Consequently, the video phone will act as a catalyst to bring people closer together, particularly friends and relatives who live far apart. One of the great frustrations of talking to someone long distance is that you feel somewhat detached from the other person because you can't see him; you have to go strictly on what you hear, and, depending on your long distance carrier, sometimes that makes for confusing, unsatisfactory conversation. But with the video phone, you will be able to read the other person's body language as well as hear his voice. The discussion will be more meaningful; you will have a better sense of what the other person believes and feels, and so you will feel closer to him. Once consumers start using the video phone, this will become abundantly clear, and it will help alleviate resistance to the concept.

3.

Thanks to the Personal Video Recorder, consumers will be able to pause a live show when they receive a phone call on their television. They will take the phone call and then hit a button to pick up the show where they left off.

4.

The video phone will change the rules of etiquette for telephone conversations. Each party will have to pay more attention to the discussion, or at least appear to. Why? The other person will be able to see you look away because you're distracted or bored. You won't be able to hide behind the anonymity of a telephone receiver. In addition, other phone habits such as doodling, eating, and playing with the household pet during a call will be considered discourteous, just as they would be if you did those things during a conservation in person. It will take people a while to adjust to the new rules—and etiquette considerations will increase the telecommunications companies' challenge to persuade consumers to adopt the video phone. However, like any new form of discourse, practice makes perfect, and the new way will become the norm before people even know it.

■ **5.**

The video phone will certainly lead to some creative uses, but none may be more original than in the area of sexual relations. It's not hard to predict that phone sex—a 1990s trend so popular that it was even practiced by a U.S. president—will only escalate. The imagination boggles at the possibilities, but a good upbringing prevents me from offering specifics. I will say that I hope people remember that recordings can be made of any and all activities. (The Fox network has probably already scheduled a "Video Phone Sex" special for the year 2008.) Staying with romance, many couples will first lay eyes on each other during a video phone call, initiated after "meeting" in an online chat room. The video phone will be a safe and fast way for two people to check each other out before they decide to go on a date.

■ **6.**

The video phone will also prompt more companies to allow their workers to operate from home, because it will make it easier for them to communicate with the office. As I noted in prediction #2, people communicate better if they can see each other. Consequently, business executives will be less concerned about jeopardizing company efficiency if they permit some of their employees to work from home. The video phone will have a powerful impact on the telecommuting movement, which began to grow rapidly in the 1990s.

■ 7.

An early success story of the video phone: a feature that will allow you to watch a TV show and talk to a friend in a second pop-up window on screen. The two parties will be able to discuss their reactions to the show—face to face—while the show is still running. For example, two football fans in different parts of the country could talk to each other about what play will be called next and then actually see each other's reactions as the play unfolds. It will be just like having your friend in the room with you. Needless to say, this picture-in-picture feature will be greatly popular with teenagers. If you haven't been around one lately, don't ask why.

■ 8.

Another early success story: In addition to sending a text e-mail, consumers will have the option of sending a video or audio e-mail to friends and loved ones. WebTV, the Internet TV set-top box from Microsoft, began offering the audio e-mail feature in 1998. (WebTV owners could also send a "video capture" via e-mail—a still picture from a live video that was showing on the TV screen—but at the time of the writing of this book, WebTV had yet to launch a true video e-mail.) The audio e-mail was a big step forward, but most WebTV owners had difficulty figuring out what was required to use it. (For starters, you needed to buy a separate microphone.) Consequently, the feature was rarely used. However, the video phone setup of the future will have a user-friendly microphone and a camera built in.

9.

The caller I.D. feature has been one of the most popular advances in phone technology over the last several years. The feature is based on the simple but undeniable truth that Americans want to be able to screen their calls. However, one drawback to caller I.D. is that it requires you to physically get up and walk over to the phone to read the telephone number of the person who's calling. With many phones connected to answering machines, which are set to take the call after a certain number of rings, it doesn't give you much time to walk over and check out the number before picking up the receiver. Consequently, many consumers do not even look at the number until they begin to lift the receiver to their ear. The caller I.D. of Interactive TV will eliminate that problem forever. When someone receives a call while watching television, the phone number of the person (or telemarketer) calling will flash on the screen on the first ring. The consumer can hit a button on his remote control and have a video phone call on screen—or ignore the call and let his answering machine pick it up. Of course, the caller will be able to leave a "video message"—a live video reminding his friend to call back.

10.

The novelty of the video phone will lead to an initial increase in the total number of phone calls in the United

States (particularly after consumers get over their social nervousness of knowing the caller can see them). People *love* toys, and they want to use them over and over after they bring them home. The video phone won't be any different.

CHAPTER NINE

I Played *Mortal Kombat* with Saddam Hussein!

Games played with the ball are too violent for the body and stamp no character on the mind.
—*Thomas Jefferson*

I must confess that the fine art of playing video games is not among my God-given talents. After I enter a video arcade or sit down in front of a video game console such as Sony's PlayStation, my hands suddenly become special effects from a David Cronenberg film. Extra thumbs and fingers shoot up in all directions; they pulsate, become larger, and seem ready to explode at any moment. The effect is undeniable. I couldn't hit a thug in the game *Doom* if I threw the console at the screen. I am much better at those games with the ball that Mr. Jefferson alluded to.

Heaven knows, I have faithfully tried to conquer video game after video game, starting in the late 1970s with *Space Invaders*. For those of you who were not around during that time, *Space Invaders* would challenge today's Starbucks in the category of urban proliferation. The game was in every shopping mall, pizza place, and bar in the United States; only shut-ins and certain aluminum siding salesmen managed to escape its grasp. *Space Invaders,* which seemed to have been designed by NASA scientists after the rudimentary and mind-numbing *Pong,* featured several rows of squat, little invaders that descended from the top of the screen to the bottom. The point of the game was to kill every invader before the top row reached the end. The skill needed to accomplish this task was minimal, but I will never forget the humiliation of once getting wiped out on the first screen. Oh, the shame of it all.

Over the years, though, I have continued to play video games despite my inadequacies; no red-blooded American male with an ounce of competitiveness can resist the challenge. I've watched the industry make extraordinary improvements in the storylines and graphics—they have to be seen to be believed. Consequently, the games have become more real than life itself for millions of teenagers—and even for many adults who suffer from arrested development. This, of course, has led to a national debate over their impact on our culture and our collective psychological state. Video games have been blamed for everything from the tragedy at Columbine High School to a higher incidence of drug use. Blaming video games and the media as a whole for violent behavior has always seemed a bit odd to me. History's most notorious acts of irrational violence occurred long before there was a television or a video game. Was Jack the Ripper influenced by the media? Was Genghis Khan?

Or Vlad the Impaler? Could there be *other* reasons that people commit senseless acts of violence, and always have?

Still, there's no denying that today's games have become an integral part of the lives of many young people. The games are so much fun—and so realistic—that they offer a refuge from the daily pressures of being a kid. Today's video game player enters another world when he turns on his console, and he doesn't come out until the game is over. When you contemplate some of the things that are happening in our world— and the drastic means of escape taken by some teenagers and adults—maybe the video game is not such a bad thing.

Social commentary aside, the video game is about to become even more pervasive and powerful in our society. Interactive TV, with its digital pictures and lightning-fast connections to the Internet, will allow companies to develop new games that will dazzle the eye and stimulate the mind as never before. The graphics will become so realistic that viewers will have difficulty separating an animated character from the real thing. The ability to interact with the games—and compete against friends and strangers around the world via the Net—will draw people even deeper into a fantasy world. If you think teenagers are transfixed by today's games, you ain't seen nothing yet. The virtual reality of tomorrow's games will be a powerful lure for both kids and adults. By clicking on your TV's remote control, you will be able to leave your cares behind and play with your favorite football players and action heroes. The images on screen will seem so authentic that you might even imagine they have come to your home at your personal invitation.

It's hard to describe the future of video games without

sounding like the narrator of a Ray Bradbury story. After all, can I be serious in suggesting that a person could play a game of *Mortal Kombat* against Iraqi President Saddam Hussein—while the dictator is sitting in his bunker? Well, if the Butcher of Baghdad owned an Interactive TV set-top box, the answer is yes. Sony's PlayStation 2 and Sega's Dreamcast, two Internet-based game consoles already in stores, offer a sneak peek at the technology that lies ahead. Early consumer reaction, which borders on mass hysteria in some circles, also hints at the emotional power of interactive gaming. The debate has just begun over whether video games have an improper influence over unformed minds.

It's a Dream

PlayStation 2 (PS2), which was introduced in Japan in March 2000 and was scheduled for launch here later in the year, will offer several Interactive TV features in one set-top box. The early model permits you to play games, DVD movies, and CD music on your TV. But in the year 2001, Sony is expected to add a cable modem that will enable players to log onto a broadband digital network where you can download games and play against other PS2 owners. (So now you know what to buy Saddam Hussein for Christmas.) Early PS2 titles include *Gran Turismo 2000,* an auto racing game, and *Exterminator,* which Sony's PlayStation web site refers to as a "Panic Action" game. (It does seem likely that, if you were playing a game called *Exterminator,* panic would be your constant companion.)

PS2's images are so vivid and life-like that they look as if they were lifted from one of today's Hollywood movies—except that game characters look more human than some of today's Hollywood actors, particularly those who have made undernourishment an art form. Lara Croft, the beautiful heroine of PlayStation's *Tomb Raider* series, seems as alive as any actress walking the streets of Sunset Boulevard; in fact, her facial mannerisms convey a greater acting range than some. Characters such as Lara are set against landscapes that offer extraordinary detail, such as puffs of smoke coming from the exhaust pipes of automobiles. The realism can be further enhanced by adding a Dual Shock 2 analogue controller that vibrates at key moments during the game to convey a sense of action. The only thing that's missing is the ability to jump into the screen and become a participant. The early buzz for PS2 was so loud that its web site had to shut down for a while before its Japanese unveiling—the site was getting 500,000 hits a *minute.*

In 1999, the launch of Sega's Dreamcast had precipitated a similar frenzy. Like PS2, Dreamcast is a game player that features realistic designs and characters as well as a modem for surfing the Net. In Japan, thousands of people began assembling in lines on the eve of the first day the $199 product went on sale. Within four hours, Dreamcast had sold out. And in the United States, Sega sold 514,000 Dreamcast consoles in the first two weeks. To put this in perspective: Dreamcast took in $97 million in U.S. sales on day one. By comparison, *Star Wars: The Phantom Menace,* the hottest movie of 1999, generated $28 million in ticket receipts on its first day.

The interactive video game has already cast a spell on millions of people, and the technology is still in its infancy.

Games eventually not only will provide a virtual experience but will act as a social catalyst to bring people together. In the spring of 2000, for instance, Sega unveiled the Sega Dreamcast Network, which permitted players to play Dreamcast games against others at a Sega-sponsored web site. "Sega is 100 percent committed to expanding and enhancing the game play experience for consumers via the Dreamcast network, and in the process, building a community where gamers can share ideas, communicate and play outstanding games," said a company publicist.

Dreamcast and PlayStation 2 are expected to be joined in the market by similar Internet-based consoles from Nintendo and Microsoft. The industry has concluded that interactive gaming has unlimited potential, and its top players are elbowing each other to get the biggest slice of the pie. Yuta Sakurai, an analyst for Normura Securities, a Japanese investment firm, says that total worldwide video game machine sales will grow from the current 100 million units to 170 million units by the year 2005.

Predictions

■ *1.*

Internet-based video game consoles such as PlayStation 2 and Dreamcast will revolutionize the video game industry. The games, which offer more realistic designs and intricate stories, will attract a whole new audience of adults. The video game will no longer be considered just a pastime for teenagers.

■ **2.**

Interactive video games will capture such a wide audience that they will attract the best actors, directors, and producers in Hollywood. The money will be too good to pass up.

■ **3.**

Hollywood's interest in the category will lead to the development of universities for game producers, similar to schools for aspiring filmmakers. Video game schools will teach students how to create and design games as well as provide strong storylines. In September 2000, the University of California–Irvine actually kicked off an Interdisciplinary Gaming Studies Program. Its course offerings explore the growing role of video games in American culture, as well as teach students the technical skills to program and design the games. The university is building a laboratory that will house a dozen computers, a library of games, and game consoles. "It's a great idea because when you think about it, interactive entertainment is going to be to the next century what television and motion pictures were to the last century," Rusty Rueff, senior vice president of human resources at gamemaker Electronics Arts, told the *Wall Street Journal.*

■ *4.*

The success of interactive games—and Interactive TV—will lead to a wave of new interactive media. Consumers will have become comfortable with the concept of interacting with entertainment. Therefore, they will be more interested in watching shows and movies that enable them to participate.

■ **5.**

For instance, the studios will begin to develop interactive movies to compete with interactive video games. The movies will permit the viewer to interact with the characters and influence the outcome of a story. A DVD of a popular film could have two versions on the disc; one would be the original movie, and the other would be an interactive version, which would enable the viewer to change how the film unfolds and ultimately ends. For instance, the viewer could choose how an action hero reacts in a tight spot by selecting one of three options: (1) Fight, (2) Run, or (3) Talk His Way Out of the Problem. After selecting the preferred option, the viewer would see the scene in which the character performs in the manner requested. The viewer's selection would then dictate how the next several scenes played out. This prediction may happen sooner than you might think; many of today's DVD movies offer scenes of alternative endings.

■ **6.**

The networks will create companion video games for many prime-time shows. After a viewer watches a popular action show, for instance, she could play the interactive version on her PlayStation or Interactive TV set-top box. The network-produced game will include a link to a web site that will promote the actual show. The game will also include interactive "triggers" that will permit you to buy related products and services as you play.

CHAPTER 10

Television Is Watching Us

Nothing else in the world—not all the armies—is so powerful as an idea whose time has come.
—*Victor Hugo*

Men have become the tool of their tools.
—*Henry David Thoreau*

In the 1960s, television became the most powerful medium in our country, eclipsing the newspaper, radio, and the cinema. Presidents were elected because they looked better on TV than their opponents. Football surpassed baseball as the nation's number one sport because it also looked better on the tube. Image was everything.

Television's growing influence on the nation was not well received by all. The comedian Ernie Kovacs, one of the great pioneers of early TV, said that television was called a "medium" because it was neither rare nor well done. Kovacs, of course, was joking, but his remark echoes what has been the prevailing wisdom among social critics for fifty years: that television is superficial, insubstantial, and frequently disposed to appealing to the lowest common denominator. Admittedly, after observing television's recent infatuation with shows that have *Millionaire* in the title, it becomes more difficult to put up a defense. I half expect to see NBC rename its evening news program *NBC Nightly News with Millionaire Tom Brokaw.*

But, nonetheless, I think that television has been unfairly criticized. For every millionaire show, there's an *E.R.* For every *When Animals Strike Back,* there's a *Simpsons,* a *Sopranos,* a *Seinfeld.* Television is truly a democratic institution—it has something for everyone. It offers instant gratification for all moods, interests, and desires. That's why television became more powerful than any other medium. The first thing that many people do when they come home at night is turn on the TV.

Universities and other well-meaning organizations have spent millions of dollars to investigate whether television has an impact on our culture. You would think that they would consider investing those funds in more mysterious pursuits, such as why people in grocery store lines never look for their wallets until the cashier asks for their money. Nevertheless, the studies come out every few months or so and, to no one's great surprise, they conclude that television is very influential.

But there will be a real need to examine the role of television when Interactive TV becomes a fixture in millions of homes. ITV will dramatically change how we watch TV, how we use the Internet, how we shop, how we communicate with others, and even how we decide where to work, thanks to the video phone. In short, it's going to change how we live. If you think television is powerful now, oh boy, just wait. ITV will make our lives so convenient and enriching that we will become even *more* addicted to the tube. People will spend more hours at home—and they will be able to spend more quality time with their families, because ITV's home networking feature will reduce the time spent on household chores. After a few months of having Interactive TV in their homes, Americans will wonder how they ever managed without it.

The Other Side

There is, however, a cautionary tale to tell. I will refrain from mouthing the usual Orwellian cliches, but the people who run television networks and ITV companies will know nearly everything about you. They will know which shows you watch, which products you order, the number of phone calls you make and to whom you make them. Each time you make a selection on your remote control, your digital set-top box will collect that data and send it to the powers-that-be. Philosophers say a person can be defined by the sum of his or her choices. If that's true, your ITV company will have a pretty good idea of who you are.

WebTV, the Internet TV company owned by Microsoft, has been gathering data on its customers for several years. Every night, WebTV downloads its subscribers' web site and TV viewing choices. They then share the information with advertisers so that they can more effectively target their messages.

"We have a department that does nothing but look at the information," former WebTV president Steve Perlman said in 1998. "The balance is providing advertisers with useful information while still protecting our subscribers."

This is not a new development—after all, nearly all businesses gather personal data on us, such as our income level, age, and marital status. In addition, many web sites build individual profiles by placing what is known as "cookies" on your PC when you visit the site. This enables the dot.com to record everything you do when you're there. If you searched for a naughty picture of Pamela Anderson Lee, they've got a record of it.

But never before in our nation's history has a single entity been the keeper of so much sensitive information. You could argue that even the government would not know as much about us. There's no evidence to suggest that ITV companies will use this information to cause harm to an individual. However, it's hard to ignore the possibility that a rogue employee, from time to time, would release personal data for less than altruistic reasons. The potential for abuse has prompted a California state senator to introduce legislation preventing cable and satellite TV companies from tracking and selling records of what people watch.

"It's nobody's business whether you're watching *Wall Street Week* or *Who Wants to Be a Millionaire* on network television or whether you're ordering *Ishtar* and *Halloween III* on pay-per-view," says Senator Debra Bowen (D). (I certainly agree with Bowen that you don't want anyone to know that you paid good money to watch *Ishtar* on PPV.)

The senator's bill would subject an ITV company to a $500 fine for every time it released viewing data without the customer's permission. Current California and federal law permits TV companies to sell a subscriber's personal information for "legitimate" business purposes. However, Bowen notes that video stores and libraries are prohibited from releasing customer records to third parties without the customer's permission. She says an Interactive TV company shouldn't be any different.

"I have the same privacy concerns with this technology (ITV) that I do with online companies that leave cookies on people's computers so marketing companies . . . can track people's Web surfing habits and build profiles on them," Bowen says.

Bowen introduced her privacy bill in February 2000. As I write these lines, it's unclear if it will make it through the California Legislature. The debate is just getting started, however. I predict that the erosion of individual privacy will be one of the top issues of the 2004 presidential race.

As more Americans go online—and allow high-tech companies to record their every move—concerns will grow that an individual's "personal profile" could wind up in the wrong hands. Lawmakers will eventually bow to constituent pressure and pass legislation similar to Bowen's proposal that would assess a fine against a company that releases a customer's personal data without the customer's permission. But how does Congress or a state legislature address the greater issue that the company has acquired the information in the first place? Will consumers be satisfied that it's illegal to release it—knowing that it's sitting there in a database like a time bomb? Will they be comfortable knowing that one company has a record of every occasion they watched *The Playboy Channel* or entered a chat room for "Swinging Singles"? Will they even want that company to know that they are more likely to watch Fox than PBS?

Interactive TV could be the greatest technological advance in our nation since the invention of television itself. But ITV companies that wish to be welcomed into the nation's living rooms may first need to ensure consumers that what they see there will *stay* there.

About the Author

PHILLIP SWANN is an Internet expert with over twenty years' experience in publishing, marketing, advertising, and public relations. He is currently the editor of SonyStyle.com. He founded *TV Online,* the nation's first magazine devoted to Interactive TV, and is the former publisher and editor of *Satellite DIRECT* and *Satellite ORBIT* magazines. He has appeared as an expert on several national television and radio shows, including *The Larry King Show, NBC Nightly News with Tom Brokaw,* and CNN's *Digital Jam.* He lives in California.